KAMTA

A PRACTICAL KAMITIC PATH FOR OBTAINING POWER

Derric Moore

Published by: Four Sons Publications

Contact: 1 SőL Alliance Co.
                   P.O. Box 596
                   Liberal, KS 67905-0596
                   www.1solalliance.com

Includes Index
Cover art and Illustrations by: Derric "Rau Khu" Moore
Artwork: Public Domain
Photos courtesy of Dreamstine.com

ISBN: 978-0-615-46851-8

Publication Date: March 25, 2011

Printed in the United States of America

CONTENTS

ACKNOWLEDGMENTS

THANK YOU Nebertcher - God, Lord of All and Supreme Being of Everything. You who are everything I know and everything that is a mystery to me. Thank you for creating the beautiful and sacred Universe around me, and the beautiful and sacred universe within.

Thank you netcharu, great guardian spirits to us all who protect the mysteries of God. Thank you for encouraging me and revealing to me the importance of group energy that is needed to create change. Thanks for your legends, stories, folkloric myths and all your mystical manifestations that have helped me to see that leaders are great focus points for group objectives, but some things we don't need to wait for a leader. Some things we can do for ourselves by simply working with others of a like mind. It is through team effort and working with others we are able to improve the quality of life for all.

To my aakhu, thanks Aunt Liz, Uncle James, Grandpa Moore, Granddad, Gram and all of you who have helped me to understand the significance of a family. Thank you for accepting my petition for cultural change and supporting me to bring about healing. Thanks to those long and forgotten whose blood flows through me and have called me to tell your story.

To my family and friends, thanks for your love, support and agreeing to disagree until further notice.

Thanks to my wife, daughter, son and grandchildren, and in-laws who have taught me about myself as I have learned more about you.

A special thanks to Ms. B, Papa Raul, Ms. Smith, and Iya, whose teachings I am still reflecting upon to this day years later.

Thank you all you teachers whose paths I have crossed, who have helped me in one way or another.

INTRODUCTION

The Spirit of Kamit among Us

History teaches us that whenever two cultures encounter each other through conquest. The dominant culture usually extracts from the subjugated the more constructive aspects of its culture. As a result, the people who have been subdued will either willingly or by force adopt the dominant culture as their own, while ignoring their cultural significance, but the culture of the subdued will not go quietly. It will continue to survive (even as an afterthought) until its people has no further need of it. If ever the needs of the subjugated people become so greater that the culture of the dominant people cannot and will not provide. The culture or the spirit of the subjugated people will rise. This *Spirit* is the Spirit of Kamit, not just the ancient Egyptians, which has inspired archeologists, historians and scholars alike to investigate and study her history. No. Ancient Egypt is just the tail end and the last of the black civilizations that were built along the Nile. The *Spirit of Kamit* lies much deeper and its roots reached deep into present-day Sudan.

It is this Spirit that has calls out to all of its biological descendants and all whom have been culturally influenced. To come to her aide and fight against the present confederacy led by the followers of evil. Don't be fooled. This is not a fight based upon the color of one's skin or the difference in beliefs. It is a war about the future of the culture of humanity and knowledge of Self. If there is one thing that science fiction has taught us, is that a horrific future will be created if we choose to chart our lives without any divine assistance. That future is amongst us now, as evident by the numerous changes occurring worldwide. It is this change that is motivating people from all walks of life to move beyond religious fervor that has contributed to the global threat everyone is feeling. And, embrace some type of spiritual practice soon to restore balance back into one's life.

The purpose of this book is to present a practical alternative approach to the Kamitic spiritual tradition, which is the oldest and most influential spiritual tradition that has weathered the ravages of time. Why? It is because we are all in need of a healing. Therefore, what you are about to read within these pages is based upon my personal experience and is my truth. If anyone chooses to disagree with what is presented within these pages. They have every right to do so, but it will not change nor deny me of the experience, which has been totally unique to me. My intention of presenting what I have experience in this informal format is to help you to explore the mystery of God that is waiting for you.

Because everything that exist is composed of energy and energy moves through frequencies and vibrations, "accelerated learning" techniques have been incorporated in this book to help you to learn faster and remember what you have learned. Each chapter begins with a proverb. Following the text is a list of study questions, along with exercises, where you will be asked to make aloud, verbal declarations, along with various gestures, etc. In order to make a strong impression upon your subconscious, which will send a message to God about what it is that you want.

Although this book is written specifically for adherents who feel they have been *called* to follow the Kamitic path. Anyone and everyone that is on some path for spiritual truth can benefit and use it to find the path that their ancestors had laid before them.

With that being said, I dedicate this book to you. May we meet in KAMTA and bring back the peace, prosperity and purity associated with Osar into our lives. This is my hope and dream for us all.

- Derric "Rau Khu" Moore

CHAPTER 1

What Does It Mean to Be Made In the Image of God?

All is within your Self. Know your most inward self and look for what corresponds with it in nature.

Kamitic Proverb

It is a beautiful thing to be able to move from just believing in God, to knowing God. The difference between the two is that when you believe in God you simply repeat what you have heard, been told or read about God. You say that God is omnipresent, omniscient and omnipotent, because that is what you have been taught but when you know God. You know that God is omnipresent because you have received assistance from strangers that that you could only classified as being divine assistance. When you know God, you see that God is omnipotent because doors that were previously closed are now open. When you know God, you know that God is omniscient or "all-knowing" because you have witnessed situations that were considered impossible by human standards to resolve, miraculously made possible.

The difference between believing and knowing is based upon personal experience, but how can you experience God who face you have not physically seen, voice you have never heard and hands you have not touched? The answer is by going beyond the physical and entering the spiritual reality within, which is where God resides in all sentient beings. In other words, in order for man and woman to tap into his or her divine potential we have to learn how to access the other side of reality – the spiritual realm – intuitively, which ties into our destiny.

This was a truth that I had to learn the hard way. because I was told as a child that I was supposed to be a preacher like my father, but not knowing anything about what a true preacher does. I rebelled every way I could. I can still remember the fury I had when I was punished at church (by other adults whom knew my parents) and told the reason why I was being reprimanded for my behavior (more so than others) was because, "God's plan" was me to be a preacher. But, the very idea of being a preacher, spending all my time at church and receiving charity or donations by working as a televangelist for my service, was clearly out of the question. Even though I was very fascinated by mystical practices and spiritual traditions, I fought my calling. It wasn't until the mid-1980s when the crack cocaine epidemic hit my hometown Detroit, Michigan, that my destiny began to unfold before me.

In an attempt to escape the onslaught that claimed the lives of many young people through either drugs or drug-related crimes, I tried to implement the spiritual practices I had learned in my youth, and failed miserably. Though, I had managed to survive the era by steering away from conflict. I noticed that I had become a very hardened young man and if provoked, I could become very violent. Seeing that anger, anguish, fear and worry could easily make me destructive to others and myself, made me realize that prayer was not enough to keep these negative emotions in check. And that suppressing them was not going to work either. This deeply disturbed me and made me angry with God because it appeared that we are all in a lose-lose situation. That's when I had my first spiritual encounter and was inspired to learn how the ancient Egyptians tapped into the power of God.

For over ten years, I read and studied every book that I could find about the ancient Egyptians, including books on religion, mysticism, alternative medicine, etc. Initially I couldn't find anything substantial because most authors subscribed to the following beliefs: (1) that ancient Egypt was part of the Middle East. (2) The ancient Egyptians worshipped numerous deities and didn't believe in one God, and. (3) the ancient Egyptian religion revolved around death. This also encouraged me to embrace conspiracy theorists.

I left home and decided to study under the tutelage of a woman who had been practicing an Egyptian-derived religion for over 13 years. She followed the philosophical belief that many whom I had met that were followers of a Kamitic path, which was that if Blacks studied and lived a clean life. We could pull ourselves up from the bootstraps

2

and overcome the pathology that slavery created, thus becoming the rulers of our own destiny. I had a romanticized view of African spirituality because I was serious in my pursuit for knowledge and righteous living. And, I fell in love with my spiritual teacher's Afrocentric mindset, which led to us becoming romantically involved. Because I was so naïve and sincere, I didn't know if what I was being taught was right or wrong. When my commonsense begged me to inquire about something. I was basically told that I was not being "spiritual." But, after years of being with this individual and seeing these teachings not work, instead lead me down a path of despair. In which I found myself drowning in debt, living in poverty, unemployed, and homeless and on the verge of having a complete mental breakdown. I realized that this complex, elegant and wordy belief system that she taught me was wrong. This was the reason it was not helping me to overcome any of the obstacles in my path. Upon realizing this, in order to keep my sanity, I had to go through the painstakingly process of unlearning and separating the "spiritual" dream from the "spiritual" reality.

It was during this crucial period in my life, I met a number of individuals that were practitioners in various Afrospiritual traditions that helped me to find my way. Like Ms. B, a *palera* (priestess) in the Palo Mayombe religion whom I met in Philadelphia that helped to demystify spirituality for me. Then there was Ms. Smith, a fellow Detroiter who ran a candle shop that helped me to understand that spiritual abilities were gifts from God. One of the most influential people that I met was Papa Raul, an old black man from Cuba who was a babalawo in the Lucumi religion and a member of the exclusive all-male Abakua Society. Papa was unique because he used conventional wisdom to shine a light to my path. Papa taught me that spirituality is not about trying to please others. It is about establishing a relationship between you and God. Papa taught me that we all have spiritual guides and guardian spirits rather we believe in them or not. And, that all we have to do is learn how they communicate to us. The most important lesson that Papa taught me was that it was foolish to try and do what the ancient Egyptians did thousands of years ago, because what worked for them pertained to only to them at the time. He told me that it is more important to focus upon understanding the concepts and

3

principles than upon copying, imitating and mimicking another's culture.

Because the process of unlearning the philosophical teachings I had adopted was so arduous and long. I had begun to lose interest in my original quest and then I met Iya (Mother) an Oshun priestess from the Ifa tradition of Nigeria. Iya was a seer and without knowing much about me. She explained to me my life story and told me why I had experienced everything that I had up until this point. She told me that everything from me being taken advantage of to the spiritual confused state that I was presently in was all due to me refusing to accept my calling.

"I am supposed to be a preacher?" I asked.

As if I had asked the question aloud or she knew what I was thinking, Iya explained that the older people in my life told me that I was supposed to be a preacher because a preacher was the only vocation that most could relate to at the time. She told me that a preacher in the Afro-American (African American and Afro-Caribbean) community fulfills several roles because they are supposed to be shamans.

"No. You are supposed to be a shaman," she calmly said.

I remembered the day she revealed this news to me. I felt like the floor had just fallen beneath me as my heart dropped. I questioned at first, what she had told me but I knew deep down it was true. It made perfect sense and when I thought about how I observed preachers in my youth. Like shamans, preachers were "called," they performed various healings and performed other duties like shamans in tribal societies, but I still didn't want to be a preacher. The thought of preaching to people for donations or having a storefront church with only five members, including myself disturbed me, because it always made me wonder were these individuals "called" to be preachers. If you were "called" to do a particular thing would you have to struggle and live in poverty as I had seen so many so-called preachers do? Iya hearing my concern told me that just because people are "called" do not mean they are supposed

4

to become preachers. The "Calling" she explained to me has different meanings in every culture. In Afro-Diaspora thinking, when one is called. It means that they are being called to use their gifts, skills and talents to serve God by improving the lives of others. An individual that has good oratory skills might be called to speak for those who cannot express themselves politically. An individual with powerful singing voice might be called to sing music to lift the spirits of others. An individual with a strong desire to understand the human physiology might be called to be a physician or surgeon and so on. This is because the calling is meant to help us to use our gifts, skills and talents for more than a materialistic purpose. I didn't understand how this could occur but Iya told me that when an individual does not accept their calling they are imbalanced. The reason is because they are either materialistic or too spiritual. This leads to them not having any peace. Summarizing her point, she told me that we are all called to fulfill a specific task on the planet. It is reason why we were born and I was born to be a shaman and to follow the *Kamitic Way*.

Iya told me to stop running my destiny and recommended that I read James Hall's *Sangoma: My Odyssey into the Spirit World of Africa,* but I was spiritually burned out. I was tired of reading and even though I heard what Iya had told me. I didn't heed her gentle warning, because I didn't want to be a shaman either. I didn't know much about what a shaman does. What I did know was that shamans were wounded healers. They helped others after overcoming spiritual, emotional and/or physical illnesses themselves, but as fate would have it, it seems. Several years after talking to Iya, I became mysteriously ill. Slowly my health deteriorated. I couldn't walk any stairs. Then suddenly I could not walk a few feet, later I couldn't stand for a long period of time, until finally, I was bedridden. I was in a horrible situation and because of my health I ended up losing my job. Fortunately, I had a little bit of money saved up but it didn't last long. Then, it happened, I became deathly ill and almost died in two separate occasions.

It was while lying on the gurney and listening to other patients in the hospital plea for death to rescue them from their suffering that I discovered God. Having nothing to lose, I began to trust in God and follow the insight given to me through my ancestors, which I wrote

5

about in my first book *MAA AANKH Volume I: Finding God the Afro-American Way, by Honoring the Ancestors and Guardian Spirits*.

I also tried to show how an imbalance occurred in my life and how I was able to restore order it by reconnecting with God. Written from a memoir perspective, I reveal the common trappings that many searching for "spiritual truth" fall into because of lack of knowledge of Self and a weak relationship they have with God. In *Kamta: A Practical Kamitic Path for Obtaining Power*, I have provided more details, instructions and practical applications, so that anyone having problems can reconnect back to God the way I had done.

So, if you are ready to conquer your anger, prejudices, old traumas, and all of the other negative emotions that have controlled your life. If you are ready to stop living in fear and worrying about what the future will bring, instead of creating the future you want. If you are ready to clear your mind of mental garbage, that is keeping you from tapping into the power of God and succeeding in all areas of your life. If you are ready to take responsibility of your actions, so that you can get out of the rut and experience some positive change. I invite you to cross the threshold and prepare yourself to receive the gift of the Spirit.

CHAPTER 2
What is Kamta?

If you would build something solid, don't work with wind: always look for a fixed point, something you know that is stable... yourself.

Kamitic Proverb

In the Beginning

According to the "Out of Africa" theory that is prevalent amongst anthropologists today, that the oldest fossil remains that have been recovered indicate that the first Homo sapiens lived in Africa around 4.4 million years ago[1], thus making Africa the birthplace of humanity. Based upon a study conducted around the globe on genetic markers, about 100,000 years ago these human beings began to migrate out of Africa and settle around the world stages[2].

It is not known why these early human migrated out of Africa. What is known is that the modern humans and Neanderthals evolved from a common ancestor who lived in Africa 700,000 years ago. One group of descendants migrated out of Africa and into Neanderthal, while another stayed in Africa and wandered throughout the African continent. Life for these early human beings one can imagine was very difficult because they were preyed upon by wild animals and had to fight the elements. Eventually, according to archeological research these early human beings learned how to build crude housing structures and create crude tools to gather food hunt and protect themselves. In time, they began to band together and create families and later tribal clans.

---

[1] Associated Press, *Oldest human remains found in Ethiopia*, New York Post, October 1, 2009

[2] John Roach, *Massive Genetic Study Supports "Out of Africa" Theory*, National Geographic News, February 21, 2008. *"Out of Africa" Theory*, National Geographic News, February 21, 2008.

As human beings continued to scatter across the earth, a number of these people in Africa migrated around the Nile River. These ancient Africans that settled along the north-flowing Nile River began at first by building small city-states in Kush (present day Sudan) and marking their accomplishments by erecting around 32 small pyramid structures. Centuries later these ancient Africans continued migrating along the Nile River and towards the Mediterranean Sea. In time they began to lay the foundation and discover the country we know today as ancient Egypt.

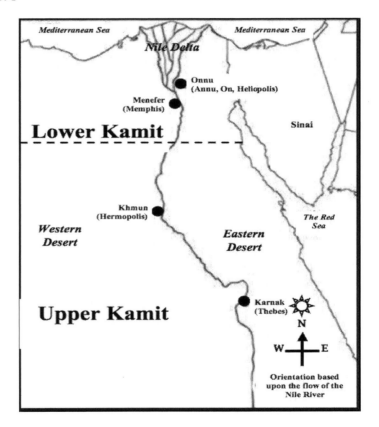

The history of ancient Egypt is long, marvelous and epic who's chronology can be divided into 30 dynasties and several periods from as early as 5000 – 3150 B.C.[3] to around 90 – 100 A.D., when the Greeks, Romans and later Arab rulers seized control of the country. There are a number of reasons why this classic civilization stood for such a long period of time. One is because the Nile River, which consisted of two major tributaries, called the White Nile and the Blue Nile, flooded annually and created two distinct regions characterized by the color of the soil.

In the northern region where the Nile stretched its way towards to the Nile Delta and poured out into the Mediterranean Sea, the soil was barren, dry and red. So the early settlers called the country Kamit and the northern region was called Lower Kamit, while the southern region where the Nile flooded and the soil became black, fertile and rich, which naturally yielded lush vegetation and attracted all sorts of wild game was called Upper Kamit.

In order to take advantage of fertile soils in the south, the early Kamitians began noting and later recording the environmental changes that occurred in relation with the Nile River. It was by observing animal migrations and the other natural events that occurred in the skies when the Nile flooded. Along with careful observation and trial and error, that led to the creation of the solar calendar[4], which laid the foundation for the people in the Kamitic society to move from being a hunter-gather society to an agricultural society.

By eliminating the constant worry of food, the Kamitic people were able to share what they produced with others, which allowed for them to establish trade and build a strong economy. It was during this time, which became the most stable period in the history of the country (around 5000 to 3200 B.C.) Kamit marveled in greatness while

---

[3] It should be noted that during this time most of Europe and Asia were still in the Paleolithic stage around 3500 B.C.

[4] It should be noted that the Kamau around 4236 B.C.E. in order to rid themselves of using a leap year calendar, also created a sidereal calendar based upon the Dog Star Sirius. This calendar was more accurate than the solar calendar but was abandoned when the conquerors of Kamit could not comprehend it.

discovering agriculture, architecture, science, philosophy, medicine and a host of inventions. A thorough analysis of the Kamitic history, myths, legends, religions and sciences reveals that the Kamitic people credited their success to the One God. This One God or Netchar is the Supreme Being and was the original God over all other gods, which is a reference meaning that God is the *Source of Everything*. The Kamitic name of Netchar (God/Supreme Being) is *Nebertcher*, whose name literally means *Lord of Everything*.

Nebertcher in the minds of the Kamitic philosophers was literally so exalted, great, powerful and abstract. That the mere human mind could not properly understand who or what God was because, God is unimaginable and indescribable. This, however did not stop the Kamitic people from trying to understand their Creator, because like people nowadays. The Kamitic people had questions and the wanted to know, "Why are we here?" "What is our purpose?" "Why were we created?" "What is the meaning of life?" So, in response of these ageless questions the ancient philosophers created a spiritual tradition because they believed. In order for man and woman to live intelligently they had to understand Netchar and all of Netchar's laws. Netchar was later translated in Latin as "Natura" and became survives today in English as Nature and personified as Mother Nature. This spiritual tradition or mystery school became known as the *Amun Ra* spiritual tradition. The main purpose of the Amun Ra spiritual tradition was to teach man and woman:

1. How to use his and her intelligence.
2. When facing danger and adversity to be courageous and patient.
3. When in the midst of temptation, follow *maa* and be true to one self.
4. Live one's life as a sacrifice to God by aspiring to do Good or Evil.

The Kamtiic people never worshipped nature. They like many first people around the world carefully observed and studied nature because their survival closely depended upon it. It was through their careful observation it was discovered that there was a duality that existed in all things. So, Nebertcher they understood was a perfect and androgynous Being. Unlike the early Jewish and Christian philosophers that created the Story of Adam and Lilith and later Adam and Eve, to justify their ill treatment and oppression of women. The Kamitic philosophers saw in nature that man and woman were two sides of the same coin and therefore interdependent upon one another. As a result, every thing that existed in Kamitic religious thinking had an equal counterpart, because it created balance. It was this understanding that allowed women in Kamit to enjoy similar rights as men, such as the right to divorce, own property and join the priesthood. All feats that women still have not been able to enjoy freely today amongst so-called "intelligent" contemporary societies.

The Amun Ra spiritual tradition was not practiced like religions are practiced today where on a specific day. One goes to a building and pays devotion to the Supreme Being. The Amun Ra mystery system was the philosophical basis for the Osarian spiritual tradition according to the oldest religious books in the world, the *Pyramid Texts* (2400 – 2300 BC) and the *Book of Coming Forth by Day* (the so-called *Egyptian Book of the Dead,* which was used from 1500 BC to 50 BC) in comparison with the Kamitic history. The two were practiced right alongside each other similar to the way Christians venerate martyrs and saints and the Chinese practice Taoism and Shenism.

Since God was seen as an abstract, indescribable, unimaginable and infinite Being. If someone needed something they would invoke or conjure the ones closest to God for assistance, which manifested their highest ideals. This is very similar to the way angels were worked with in Judaism. The netcharu were never worshipped. For instance, if an individual was suffering from lustful behavior, they would symbolize the immoral behavior as a pig or a monstrous serpent and call upon Hruaakhuti, a great legendary warrior known for championing God's causes to assist them in overcoming the destructive habit as he overcame the beast that rebelled against God's will. The analogy was simple and in time through constant repetition of the practice would create an emotional energy encouraging them to overcoming their negative conduct. Similar to the way some Christians would call upon

11

Saint George to help them to overcome an undesirable condition similar to the monstrous dragon of medieval times.

The Amun Ra spiritual tradition was widely practiced because it wasn't just the king that was viewed as being the Son of God as archeologists claim, which was clearly a concept that was adopted by the early Christians. Everyone according to Kamitic theory was seen as a Child of God. Everyone had a patron guardian spirit that connected them to the Divine, which meant the divine potential resided within everyone regardless of their association, affiliation, ethnicity, background and gender. Everyone in Kamitic belief had his or her unique purpose in life, signified by one's abilities, skills and talents. These gifts according to Kamitic belief that were given to us by God to acquire peace, happiness, prosperity and well being on earth, while striving to fulfill our purpose in life. And this is why the Amun Ra spiritual tradition was the oldest religion of antiquity and the most widely practiced with religious centers existing as far north as Greece and far south as Kush or Nubia. Later when Christianity began to rise in popularity, Christianity was religiously syncretized with the Amun Ra religion in order to give it spiritual validity.

The Fall of Kamit

The destruction and end of the Kamit came when the Amun Ra spiritual tradition was destroyed upon the arrival of the Greeks who bastardized the Kamitic religion and renamed Kamit, Aegypt and finally Egypt. Shortly after, the Romans conquered Egypt, followed by the Arab rulers who control country to this day, but archeological evidence reveals that some time during the middle of the Kamitic Dynastic Period. A large number of people migrated out of Kamit and into the African interior. It is not known why this mass exodus happened but it is believed that it was most likely due Islamic jihads incited by zealous Arabs that reached its height around 641 AD. Two of the ethnic groups in particular that left Kamit were the Twa (the so-called pygmies of Africa) and the Hutu, who are believed to be the ones responsible for spreading the Amun Ra tradition outside of the Kamitic borders throughout the African continent[5]. In the east these people became known as Kikuyu (or Agikuyu), in the West the Yoruba and in the south as Amazulu. In Central West Africa, a number of these Bantu[6] speakers became known as the Bantu-Kongo[7] who founded the Kongo[8] Kingdom.

Although there is a vast amount of cultural evidence supporting the theory that a number of Kamitic people migrated towards the Atlantic coast, and various scholars like Sir E.A. Wallis Budge, who went against his colleagues and stated in his book *Osiris and the Egyptian Resurrection (1911)*,

> "There is no doubt that the beliefs examined herein are of indigenous origin, Nilotic or Sundani in the broadest signification of the word, and I have endeavored to explain those which cannot be elucidated in any other way, by the evidence which is afforded by the Religions of the modern peoples who live on the great rivers of East, West, and Central Africa . . . Now, if we examine the Religions of modern African peoples, we find that the beliefs underlying them are almost identical with those Ancient Egyptian ones described above. As they are not derived from the Egyptians, it follows that they are the natural

---

[5] Lecture delivered for the Minority Ethnic Unit of Greater London Council, London England, March 6-8, 1986 titled *The Nile Valley Civilization and the Spread of African Culture* by Yosef-ben Jochannan
[6] The term Bantu or Ba Ntu means "the men" or "the people" is derived from the ancient Egyptian word Nti pluralized as Ntu according to Gadalla, Moustafa. *Exiled Egyptians; the Heart of Africa.*
[7] The Bantu Kongo are an ethnic group belonging to the Bantu people, which form about 1/3 of the African continent's population.
[8] Kongo is spelled with a K instead of a C to distinguish between the Kongo civilization, which encompassed neighboring territories in modern Bas-Zaire, Cabinda, Congo-Brazzaville, Gabon and northern Angola, from colonial Congo (present-day Zaire) and the present-day People's Republic of Congo-Brazzaville. Robert Farris Thompson, *Flash of the Spirit: African and Afro-American Art and Philosophy* (New York: Vintage Books, 1984), p. 103.

product of the religious mind of the natives of certain parts of Africa, which is the same in all periods."

Since there is no solid anthropological evidence that has been recovered connecting Kamit with West Africa, the issue remains open to debate. Despite the fact that similar mummification rites, ritual observances, religious services, fetishes, cultural customs and even words have been found in West and Central African cultures.

Like the Kamitic people, the Kongo people identify themselves by their clans, village or chiefdom whose kingdom they resided under. Archeological evidence indicates that they were great agriculturist and had been working with iron for a relatively long time. Then in 1483, Portuguese merchants and Christian missionaries arrived on the shores of Africa and shortly after established trade with the Kongo people. Like most cultures when they encounter another culture with greater physical amenities, the Kongo were very impressed with the Portuguese culture and their religion. In a relatively short time a religious syncretism developed between the Kongo indigenous religion and the Christian faith in part, because the Kongo people, like their ancestors along the Nile, did not make a distinction between the secular and the sacred. This made it difficult to translate some of the Christian concepts into the KiKongo language. So words like "holy" were translated in KiKongo to "nkisi" which is, an abstract word meaning medicine or charm. The word "martyr" was translated in KiKongo to bakulu (ancestral spirits), "saints" was translated to basimbi (benevolent spirits) and "demonic spirits" were translated to bankyu (malevolent spirits). While some of the Christian missionaries denounced and objected to this mixing of traditions, they could not prevent it from occurring because it was the only way Christian concepts could be translated into the Kongo language.

Consequently, Christianity rapidly spread throughout the Kongo Kingdom and was eventually declared the official religion of kingdom, but when the demand for more slaves rose to work the fields, mines and plantations in the New World in the following decades. The BaKongo were undermined, conquered and defeated due to invasion, civil discord, slavery and war, resulting in the total fall of the Kongo Kingdom.

As a result, most (if not all) of the people from the Kongo-Angolan region taken to North America came with a working religious syncretism between their traditional religious beliefs and Christianity already intact. Since the Africans taken to North America were prohibited from speaking their own language, playing drums (a vital element in African religions), practicing their cultural traditions and congregating except for under the strict and cautious slave owner's supervision. Early African Americans like African descendants in the Caribbean and Latin America met clandestinely and began adopting various influences to fill the religious void created by slavery, in order to emotionally, spiritually and physically survive the brutal system. One of the major differences between the Africans in North America and those in the Caribbean and Latin America religiously speaking was that the medium of choice was Protestant Christianity instead of Catholicism.

The descendants from the Kongo-Angolan region that were kidnapped and brought to North America, along with other African captives, simply Africanized Protestant Christianity. By adapting and adopting westernized ideals like the Exodus, Ethiopia and Egypt and masking their beliefs in order to preserve their *"Africanness"*. This can be seen in African American beliefs and practices such as the spirituals, receiving the Holy Ghost (a form of spiritual possession), shouting (spiritual dancing), fasting for spiritual strength and inner vision (wisdom), the laying of hands, dream interpretation, etc. But, because the enslaved Africans taken to North America were prohibited from speaking their language, practicing their cultural tradition and further discouraged from exploring their mystical path. They lost the spiritual tradition that helps initiates consciously rid themselves of the destructive and negative influences (such as fears, inhibitions, guilt and other negative emotions learned through social conditioning), which psychologists have acknowledged prevents any individuals from discovering his or her true self.

Since the theological contexts were lost, the final product was an eclectic blend of practices only spoken about and used in secret perceived by the dominant culture as being backwards, silly, superstitious, foolish, devilish and evil, hence the "voodoo mentality." Fortunately, because the African beliefs, practices and values survived, by following the insight from my ancestor, I was able to use the surviving concepts and principles as a guide. To discover a very unique system that would allow anyone serious about spiritual development to reconnect with his or her ancestral past and be reborn, by following the *Rule of the Sun* through the Kamitic *Story of Ra and Oset*.

The Story of Ra and Oset

According to legend, Oset XE "Oset" was a woman that possessed words of power but wanted to know the secret name of Ra, so that she could become a divinity that was cherished in the heavens and the earth. So she devised of a plan to get the great Ra to share his secret name with her.

Every day, Ra entered and established himself upon the throne of the two horizons, Oset noticed that he had grown old, he dribbled at the mouth, his spit fell upon the earth, and his slobbering dropped upon the ground. On one particular day when this happened, Oset took the slobber of Ra and kneaded it with the earth in her hand, and made a serpent in the form of spear. She set the serpent upright before her face, but allowed it to lie upon the ground on the path so that when Ra passes by it during his journey through his kingdom, it would afflict him.

As before, Ra arose and set forth upon his daily journey and when he came across the serpent lying on the path; it bit him causing the sacred fire of life to depart from him. Ra opened his mouth and cried out, "What has happened?" and all that was with him exclaimed, "What is it?" but, Ra could not answer because his members quaked, his mouth trembled because the poison of the serpent had swiftly spread throughout his body.

Ra stated to all those who had accompanied him on his journey to tell Khepera that a dire calamity had fallen upon him, thereby preventing

16

him from continuing his journey. He exclaimed that he didn't see what ailed him or what caused the great pain and agony that he was in, nor did he know who had did it to him. All that he knew was that he had never felt pain like the pain that he was in. Ra in total disbelief that someone would dare harm him cried out that he was a prince, the son of a prince, a sacred essence that came from God. Ra cried out further that he was the son of a great one whose name was planned and as a result, he had a multitude of names and a multitude of forms and he exists in everything.

Ra further proclaimed that all heralds his coming as his father and mother utter his name, that was secret and hidden within him by the one that begat him, which he would not divulge to anyone for fear that they would have dominion over him. Ra recounted his journey by stating that he came forth to survey all that he created and it was while passing through the world that something mysteriously stung him. What was it Ra wondered. Was it fire that made him hotter than fire or water that made him feel so cold, he wondered that made his heart feel like it was on fire, his body tremble and flesh to shake with sweat.

Furious, Ra called upon all of his children to come before him and to assist him in destroying the illness, but none could heal Ra and wept heavily. When Oset appeared before the trembling king, she asked Ra, what had happened to him and was it a serpent that rose against him and bit him. She told Ra that with his power and her words she could drive the illness away.

Ra told Oset, that he was passing along my daily journey, and I was going through the two regions of my lands according to my heart's desire. In order to see that which he had created, when suddenly out of nowhere! A serpent bit him, which he did not see. Ra asked was it fire or was it water because he was colder than water and hotter than fire. Ra said that his flesh sweat, quaked, and his eyes have no strength. He told Oset that he could not even see the sky and that sweat rushed to his face as if he was in the summer.

Oset told the great Ra that she would drive the poison of the serpent away only if he would tell her his secret name, because whosoever shall be delivered by his secret name would live.

Ra responded telling Oset that *"I have made the heavens and the earth, I have ordered the mountains, I have created all that is above them, I have made the water, I have made to come into being the great and wide sea, I have made the 'Bull of his mother,' from whom spring the delights of love. I have made the heavens, I have stretched out the two horizons like a curtain, and I have placed the soul of the gods within them. I am he who, if he openeth his eyes, doth make the light, and, if he closeth them, darkness cometh into being. At his command the Nile riseth, and the gods know not his name. I have made the hours, I have created the days, I bring forward the festivals of the year, I create the Nile-flood. I make the fire of life, and I provide food in the houses. I am Khepera in the morning, I am Ra at noon, and I am Tmu at evening."*

The poison burned through Ra's body and prevented the great one from walking. Oset noticing that Ra's condition was getting worse told him that what he has said is not his hidden name and it is not driving the poison away. Again she asked that Ra reveal his secret name to her as the poison burned deeper and hotter in Ra's body. Finally, Ra consented and hid himself from the company before him and when the two could not be seen the name of Ra passed from his body into her. And when the heart of Ra came forth, Oset called her son Hru to come forth saying, "Ra hath bound himself by an oath to deliver up his two eyes" (i.e., the sun and moon). After Oset took the name of Ra she drove the poison out of Ra's body and commanded the Eye of Hru to go forth and shine outside of Ra's mouth. She enchanted "May Ra live and the poison die and the poison die and Ra live". And, that is how the great Ra who suffered the frailty and weakness of a man almost perished but was healed.

Who and What Is Ra?

To understand who and what Ra is it must be first understood that Ra is not the sun (or the so-called sun god) aten and Ra is not God[9], the Supreme Being, who in the Kamitic language is called *Nebertcher*, which means *The Lord of Everything*. The word "ra" has many meanings in the Kamitic language. It was commonly used to mean power, strength, might, energy, light, etc. When the Kamitic people wanted to distinguish between which "ra" they were referring to, they like African descendants today placed greater emphasis or stress on how the word was pronounced. For instance, if I said that this individual has power. Depending upon the conversation, it could be interpreted that I am talking about the individual having authority, respect, electricity, strength, muscle, influence, etc. This is how the Kamitic speakers used the word "ra", which is why the word "ra" was used as a prefix and suffix to form pronouns and words like Auf Ra, Ra-Ptah, Khafra, Menkaura, Asr Ra, Khnemu-ra, etc. The ancient Hebrews after living in Kamit for so long used the word "eL", which means strength, power, might, etc. the same way to form pronouns and words like EL-Shaddai, EL-ohim, EL-Olam, ang-EL, Rapha-EL, Micha-EL, Gabri-EL, and Isra-EL[10].

Generally speaking in Kamitic theology, ra is Divine grace, the chi in Chinese esotericism, prana in Indian mysticism, also called the life force or the Holy Spirit in Christian theology. Ra is the divine energy that makes up everything. This divine energy is both metaphysical and physical, and manifests itself as energy and matter, which cannot be created or destroyed only transformed. It is in the air

---

[9] Generally speaking when referring to God the Kamitic people said Neter or Netchar, which became in Latin *natura* and survives today in the English language as natural and Nature, hence Mother Nature.

[10] The ancient Hebrew it should be remember were a nomadic group that adopted and borrowed from the most influent cultures they encountered. The cultural practice of using "eL" in words came from the Kamitic people.

we breathe, the earth's magnetic field and in the light of the sun. It is in the ocean, the plants and manifests itself in our intuition and dreams. It is the force that unites us all and for our purpose it will be called *Rau* (plural for *ra*).

The various names revealed to Oset **were not gods but different attributes** of the One God who exercises Power or Authority over the Spirit or the *Rau*. For instance, **Khepe-ra** refers to God's Authority that causes things to come into existence, symbolized as the rising sun. **Ra** is God's Authority to govern life symbolized as the midday sun. **Ra Atum** is God's Authority to change anything at will. And, the secret name, **Amun Ra** is God's Authority to initiate a new beginning.

The *Story of Ra and Oset*, which has eluded many Western trained scholars, is an initiatory legend about the mysteries of death and rebirth. When understood from an allegorical perspective, Oset symbolizes our desire to want to improve our life through the power of God. The initiate that understood the tale was led to a deeper understanding about him and her self. This truth is that God is within.

It was by focusing on these concepts and principles from the story and relating them to the movements of the sun inspired by my ancestors. That led me to discover that we are a microcosm of a greater Macrocosm. In other words, the small (microcosm) universe within our physical body is a mirror reflection of a larger (Macrocosm) Universe outside of our being. Consequently, a comparison can be made between the birth, life, death and rebirth of the universe with our own evolutionary experience. It was this connection with nature that led me to discover the maa aankh.

What is the Maa Aankh?

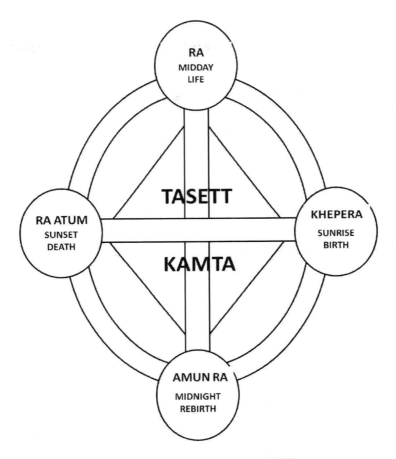

FIGURE 1: BASIC MAA AANKH

Know ye not that ye are the temple of God, and [that] the Spirit of God dwelleth in you?

1 Corinthians 3:16

The maa aankh composed of the Kamitic words maa, which means "balance, order, law, righteous, the way, cause and effect, reciprocity, etc." and aankh, which means "life, living, to swear an oath, etc," roughly translated to mean "to swear an oath to live righteous", "the order of life", "balance or righteous living", "living in moderation," etc.

all depending upon the way it is used signifying that it pertains to a system, an orderly way of doing things and/or a contract between God and man/woman. It is a cosmogram inspired by Bantu-Kongo cross and traditions that survived in North America and combined with the Kamitic philosophy.

The maa aankh indicates that everything that exist came out of a great void or the primeval waters of creation called *nyun,* the horizontal line that separates the hidden spiritual world below from the visible physical world above.

The vertical line called the *maa* creates a bridge across the nyun and mirrors everything that exists above below and vice versa. The maa establishes divine balance, law, order, justice, and reciprocity throughout the universe. Maa ensures that **reason is never eclipsed by faith**. Maa does not conform to the notion that all of our actions, attitude, behavior and circumstance that took place in our past life affect the life that we live today. It does not imply that our genes or what we did in the distant past is the reason for our fortunes or misfortunes today. Maa is based upon cause and effects or action and reaction, which means it is the beliefs we hold and decisions we make now that make us who we are today. The maa, the Kamitic philosophers state, *"links universal to terrestrial, the divine with the human is incomprehensible to the cerebral intelligence."*

It is because of the maa duality exists and expresses itself through the polar forces known as Shu and Tefnut. Shu is the upward moving force that symbolizes the natural force of expansion, heat, light, dryness, masculinity, and activity, loudness, outward, active, firm, rational, logical, mathematical and analytical. Shu is also aggression, exuberance, motion, the living, sunlight, day, upward, the heavens, top, head, studying, etc. because traditionally speaking men were more outward. Men went outside of the home and villages to hunt for food, to fight off invaders to protect the family, etc.

Tefnut is the downward moving force that symbolizes the natural force of contraction, coolness, darkness, dampness, wetness, femininity, and inertia, quiet, inward, inactive, soft, and imaginative.

Tefnut also symbolizes fatigue, selfishness, sadness, religion, philosophy, depression, weakness, meditation, the dead, the earth, downward, the night, stillness, bottom, the back, creativity, greed, sleeping, etc. because women traditionally were more inward, they stayed at home, cared for the children and family, received sperm and protected the unborn fetus (future of the family lineage) within their womb.

Together Shu and Tefnut described as being siblings and mates to indicate their interdependency upon one another are the Kamitic Yang and Yin. They represent potential change and are two sides of the same coin. Where there is one there is the other because they are the driving power of sexuality, which is the true meaning of the saying, "Behind a great man is a great woman." It has nothing to do with chauvinism but the simple fact that every cause has an effect and vice versa, Shu and Tefnut are inseparable. This is why day cannot exist without the night, the sun cannot exist without the moon, what goes up must come down, man cannot exist without woman, and good cannot exist without evil. Even in the bleakest of times there is always a glimmer of hope but at the same time in clearest of skies there's a cloud. Nothing is fixed. There is always change.

The Kamitic peoples' orientation differs from other classic civilizations because of their dependency upon the Nile River. Due to the north flowing Nile flooding and causing the southern lands to become rich and fertile, while snaking its way through the barren and red desert lands in the north before emptying out into the Mediterranean Sea. The southern region of the country became known as Upper Kamit or KAMTA[11] – the Black Lands and the northern section became known as Lower Kamit or TASETT – the Red Lands. Everything associated with Tefnut, the southern region, fertility and blackness including the female womb, the night sky, the spiritual realm, mysteries, a dark hole or fertile soil, the invisible, the "Upper" division of the Spirit, etc. corresponds to KAMTA, the mysterious and miraculous aspect that exists in the universe and deep within our being.

---

[11] When referring to the placement on the maa aankh, the word KAMTA is capitalized to distinguish it from the name of the tradition.

While everything associated with Shu, the northern section, dryness, redness, the outward energy of the traditional male, masculinity, aggressiveness, the physical realm, the known, the visible, the "Lower" division of the Spirit, etc. corresponded to TASETT, the known and mundane aspect of the universe and our being. The four discs surrounding the maa aankh are:

Khepera is the sunrise, birth, the beginning, awakening of consciousness, the eastern direction, the spring season, newborns and children, and innocence/naiveté. Refers to the physical or instinctive awareness and corresponds to the R-complex of the human brain. The color black symbolized as a scarab beetle emerging from out of dung or a hole in the earth. For simplicity purpose it will be called *The Lord of Birth and Sunrise.*

Ra is the midday sun, life, the mediation, awakened consciousness (the Left Solar Eye of Ra also called the Aakhut), the northern direction, the summer season, teenagers and young adults, emotional awareness and the beginning of rational thinking. It is the color red symbolizing caution/warning. It represents the animal instincts and corresponds to the paleo-mammalian complex. Symbolized as hovering falcon or hawk, for simplicity purpose it will be called *The Lord of Life and the Midday Sun.*

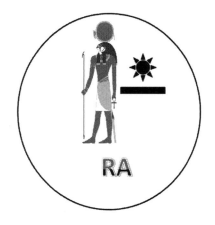

Ra Atum is the setting sun, death, the end, loss of consciousness, the western direction, the fall or harvest season, adults and elders. Wisdom acquired from self-discipline, study and age symbolized by the color white and an aging human male. It represents the neo-mammalian brain. For simplicity purpose will be called *The Lord of Death and Sunset.*

Amun Ra is the midnight sun (the sun on the other side), rebirth[12], dreaming consciousness/also the non-REM (the Right Lunar Eye of Ra also called the Aabit), spiritual awareness, receptivity, the southern direction, the winter season, stillness of mind, the color yellow symbolized as a wise man inside a youthful and vivacious body. It represents the higher functions of the neo-mammalian brain. For simplicity purpose it will be called *The Lord of Rebirth and Midnight.*

---

[12] Amun Ra who is associated with the southern region was also honored by the Kushites (southern neighbors of the Kamitic people) who tried to restore Kamit to its old glory around 1000 BC.

Once more these four discs are not to be interpreted as gods but attributes of the One God represented as the four moments of the sun – sunrise, midday, sunset and midnight (when the sun is believed to be on the other side), the evolution of the human soul – birth, life, death and rebirth; and God's Consciousness.

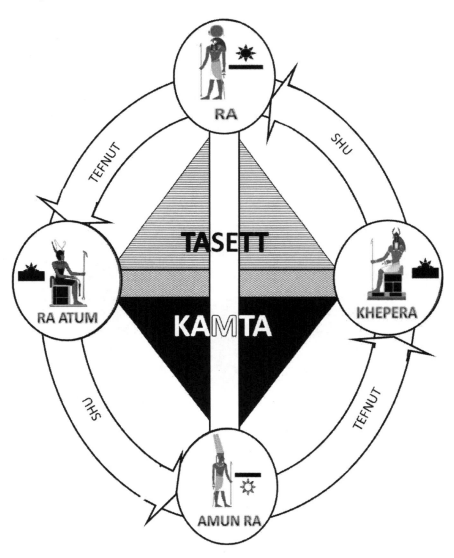

FIGURE 2: THE MAA AANKH

The maa aankh can be seen everywhere because it symbolizes our universe and marks where TASETT meets KAMTA. It also signifies where the desert meets the fertile soil. Where land meets the vast ocean, where the city meets the cemetery, or where the physical meets the spiritual realm. It marks where two distinct worlds meet, where the visible meets the invisible, man meets woman, the linear and rational meets the spatial and abstract. It notes where the living meets the honorable dead and, where man and woman meet God.

Generally speaking, the maa aankh indicates that just like everything in our universe is given its time and place in the grand scheme of things, and is kept in balance, harmony and order due to the evolution of the Sun. Man and woman's life is kept in maa due to the evolution and integrity of his and her soul, because the human being is made in the image of God.

Study Questions

1. What is the name of God in the Kamitic language and the secret name that was revealed to Oset?
   Nebertcher, which means *The Lord of Everything* and the secret name revealed to Oset was Amun Ra – which means the Hidden Ra.

2. What is the Rau?
   Rau is the Divine Energy, the Holy Spirit, divine grace, luck, power or simply the Spirit that manifests Itself as the visible, physical realm and the invisible, spiritual realm, understood to be TASETT and KAMTA.

3. What is TASETT?
   TASETT is the name the ancient Kamitic people used to describe the arid, red lands of the north, which was also called Lower Kamit, because of the north flowing Nile River. Metaphorically, TASETT symbolizes because of its red color, the visible, physical realm, that which is known (or learned based upon one's physical senses), the sciences of the earth, the

known, the solid earth, city/villages, the land of the living, etc. It is the visible, physical, material (matter) aspect of Rau.

4. What is KAMTA?
    KAMTA is used to describe the fertile, black lands of the south, which was also called Upper Kamit because of the north flowing Nile River. Metaphorically, KAMTA symbolizes the invisible, spiritual realm, the mysteries of the universe, the unknown, the night sky, the vast ocean, the sacred grove (tomb), the cemetery, the land of the ancestors and guardian spirits, etc. It is the invisible, metaphysical, spiritual aspect of Rau.

5. What is *nyun*?
    Nyun is the cosmic stuff that the universe is made out of symbolized as great void, a vast ocean full of potential like a lump of clay, just waiting to be given form.

6. What is Khepera, Ra, Ra Atum and Amun Ra? Are they gods?
    No they are not gods. These are attributes of the One God Nebertcher's Authority/Power, symbolized as the four moments of the sun – Khepera (sunrise), Ra (midday), Ra Atum (sunset) and Amun Ra (midnight) – that control and Will the Rau the Spirit of God.

7. What is Shu, Tefnut and the *maa*?
    Shu and Tefnut are the Kamitic concepts of Yang and Yin. Shu is light, heat, expansiveness, fire, positive, masculinity, etc. and Tefnut is dark, cool, contractive, water/moisture, negative, femininity, etc. Together they represent the interdependent dual forces that exist in our universe. They are the manifestation of the maa, which is the divine balance, law, order or simply the Kamitic *Way*.

8. What is man and woman's relationship to Khepera, Ra, Ra Atum and Amun Ra?
    Khepera, Ra, Ra Atum and Amun Ra are the Divine Authority that Nebertcher shares with every human. As a result, they

correlate to the evolution of man and woman's soul and state of mind: Khepera – birth, Ra – life, Ra Atum – death and Amun Ra – rebirth.

9. What is Kamta?

   The word "Kamta" (literally "Black Land" in the Kamitic language) is applied to the practice as a reference to the continent Africa as being the birthplace of humanity, the ancient builders of the Nile Valley civilization, the various Maroon cultures that developed in the throughout the Americas, the hidden spiritual realms where the honorable ancestors still reside and the higher state of mind that one can achieves through the practice.

10. What is the maa aankh?

    The maa aankh is the cosmogram composed of the Kamitic words maa, which means "balance, order, law, righteous, the way, cause and effect, reciprocity, etc." and aankh, which means "life, living, to swear an oath, etc." It is inspired by the *Story of Ra and Oset* and the Kongo Cross and serves as the philosophical basis for Kamta.

Exercise: How to Draw the Maa Aankh

Everyone and everything has a maa aankh because it is a tangible microcosm of a greater intangible Macrocosm. Most people aren't aware of their maa aankh because they have not developed the skill to focus their awareness on the invisible energies that exist, so they believe it is nonexistent. However, with a little practice, anyone can easily see, feel and eventually access their personal maa aankh and interact with others to acquire power, wisdom and wellbeing. The following seven steps for drawing the maa aankh is a simple ritual for seeing your relationship to God. Contemplation upon how the maa aankh is drawn will reveal how "thoughts" generate "action" and create "physical things."

29

Step 1: Begin by drawing from left to right a horizontal line, while saying "Nyun."

Step 2: Draw an intersecting vertical line from the bottom across the horizontal line, while saying "maa."

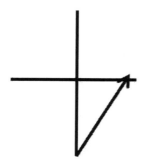

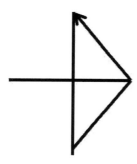

Step 3: From the arm of the vertical line draw a diagonal line to the right of the horizontal line above, while saying "Shu."

Step 4: From the right side of the horizontal arm, draw a diagonal line to the top of the vertical line, while saying "Tefnut."

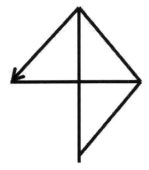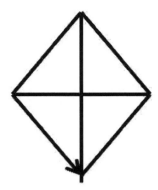

Step 5: From the top of the vertical line, draw a diagonal line to the left arm of the horizontal line, while saying "Shu."

Step 6: from the left arm of the horizontal line, draw a diagonal line to the bottom of the vertical line, while saying "Tefnut."

Step 7: Complete the maa aankh by drawing from the bottom of the diagram a counter clockwise circle connecting all of the points. While doing this say the following invocation,
"Es Khepera, Ra, Ra Atum en Amun Ra," which is a salutation to Nebertcher that means "Greetings/Hail to the One that Governs Birth, Life, Death and Rebirth."

After you have drawn the maa aankh, try seeing the maa aankh with your mind's eye. A good practice is to begin with is to see where your awareness and your temperament are at during the course of the day. For instance, observe how when you first awake from your sleep how alert you are, your mood, character, etc. Are you a morning person, irritated, etc? Observe the same thing throughout the course of the day.

The maa aankh remembers marks where the two great lands begin and end. So once you have become familiar with how to draw the maa aankh, go to the park, the woods, the riverbed, or the beach shore. If you are unable to get outside, then simply focus your attention on a plant, tree, animal, building, etc. Then while focusing your attention on these places, ask to see the maa aankh and allow any idea or thought pertaining to it to come to you freely and take note of it. Notice how events pertaining to Khepera and associated with the eastern direction all have something to do with birth, youthfulness, etc. See how events pertaining to Ra and associated with north are full of activity, strength, etc. Next watch how events pertaining to Ra Atum are associated with the west come to an end. Finally, observe how in the southern direction events that are a mystery and cannot easily be seen are associated with Amun Ra. See the maa in the center of these areas and note how it is the center of gravity for most things.

Note that the ideas that are coming to your awareness regarding these spaces are not coming from your physical senses but are "hunches." These "hunches" on the maa aankh are coming to you from the KAMTA region. More on this subject will be explained in the next chapter.

CHAPTER 3

The Three Aspects of Awareness

Know the world in yourself. Never look for yourself in the world, for this would be to project your illusion.

- Kamitic Proverb

Nebertcher is Netchar, God, No-thing, incomprehensible, indescribable and too abstract for the human mind to truly understand. God is an Infinite Spirit beyond human contact and a creative force similar to a super nova. God being the source of everything is androgynous (having no gender) yet at the same time consisting of both. The only reason we know of God is because God's fingerprints can be found everywhere. Everything that we can physically see, touch, hear, smell and taste we know was made possible through God. But God is not limited by our physical senses or what we can explain in words. All that we know is God and all that we don't know is also of God because God is *Everything*. God is Nebertcher – The Lord of Everything.

Since God is Nebertcher. God is present everywhere. When we talk about being in God's presence we are really talking about being consciously aware of God. If you are consciously aware of God and you act and behave with God on your mind. The Divine inspires everything that you do because you know God. This is the big difference between believing in God and knowing God. Throughout history we have seen plenty of examples of people that believed in God. The individuals that massacred the Amerindians, authored the Trans-Atlantic Slave Trade, slaughtered millions in China in order to maintain the opium trade in China, dropped the atomic bomb on the defeated enemies in Hiroshima, etc. all believed in God, but I seriously doubt that they knew God. This is because to know God is to know your TRUE self and understand that God dwells within you.

The Spirit of God is within us all regardless of our associations, affiliations, background, beliefs, ethnicity, and experiences, race, etc. because this is what gives us life and the energy to exist. But, we all do not function, operate and conduct our affairs through the power of God. If we did our choices, decisions and history would reflect the peace, love and joy that only come from knowing God, because if God is everywhere and God knows everything, therefore God has power over all things. Knowing God means we have the ability to accomplish any objective, fulfill every dream and overcome every obstacle in our path. The reason we all do not function and conduct our affairs through the Upper Rau is because God gives us a choice or free will, to either do things our way based upon our physical senses, or to surrender to God, the Infinite Intelligence within our being. When we begin having problems or the plans in your life are suddenly interrupted. Take it as an omen! Because it means that you are approaching danger due to you living your life based upon knowledge you have acquired through your physical senses, which is not always accurate. If what you knew were accurate then you would not be having problems. You must surrender and talk to God in order to survive.

But why is it so hard to surrender to God? One of the reasons is because there is a lot of confusion about who and what we are, as well as our connection to the Divine. In some traditions it is said that we are spiritual beings, while in other traditions it is said that we are dragged creatures of the earth with a spirit. This combined with the fact that men with their own selfish agendas and biasness have further confused the issue. By interpreting divinely inspired texts from their carnal mindset. All of this Indicates that most people find it difficult to surrender to God because, our experience has taught us that when one surrenders to anything especially something that we cannot see. We are taken advantage of because we feel that we have no control. At the root of this is fear. Fear we will have no control. Fear we will not enjoy our life. Fear that we will not have our basic needs met. Fear that we will be perceive as being crazy or lose our mind and be isolated from others – in other words fear of no love, and finally. Fear that it will lead to our

34

demise, hence the fear of death. These are all fears based upon our ignorance about the Spirit of the God and the human mind.

These fears are what prevent us from succeeding and prospering in life. To understand how we acquired these fears and how to overcome them. We need to understand what it means to be a human being.

The Kamitic understanding of the human being is similar to other systems that express the connection between the human mind or consciousness and the Universe, with some considerable differences. According to Kamitic thought, the human being is a spiritual being infused into a physical body, which means the human body is a mere shell or vehicle used specifically for physically transporting our spirit from place to place. Our spirit, which controls our being, is a complex "organism" like our physical body. It is composed of nine divisions that are all responsible for governing a specific function of our being. For convenience purposes I have grouped these nine divisions into three parts to correspond to the Western understanding of the mind. These three parts can be said to be the epicenters of the divisions that surround them. The names of these three divisions are *sahu* (physical-body conscious or subconscious mind), *ab* (spiritual heart, human conscious, conscience) and *ba* (divine conscious or unconscious mind).

Sahu – The Physical-Body Conscious

When we are born, we all come into this world with our *sahu* governing our being. Our *sahu*, which is responsible for storing our personal memories and governing all of our autonomous physiological functions, including regulating our heartbeat and directing our blood to carry oxygen throughout our body. Controls our digestion, assimilates our hormones, eliminates wastes and controls all of the vital processes of our body. Because our *sahu* governs our personal memory, it records all of our actions, behaviors and experiences associated with how we feel. It is because of our *sahu* whenever we feel pain we are motivated to move away from it. Whenever we feel pleasure on the other hand we are motivated to move towards it. Our *sahu* protects us

35

from danger and helps us to survive, which is why babies cry to alert their parents that they are hungry or feeling discomfort. As children we cry to express when we feel pain.

The drawback I learned was that our *sahu* does not give us the ability to make rational decisions. It cannot intelligently help us to determine what is good or dangerous for us, because this is not the purpose of our *sahu*. Its primary function is to help us to survive by recording, storing and releasing all of our memories. This is the reason children don't know right from wrong, but have to learn it by observing or imitating those who are older than them.

One of the ways our *sahu* helps us to survive by recording and storing all of our genetic memories at the cellular level and our learned memories at the muscular level. So, whenever we are stressed, to help us to cope with the situation, our subconscious responds by releasing these genetic memories based upon how our ancestors would have responded to the stressful situation. For specifics on how to deal with the actual stressful issue, it releases the memory that is the most closely associated with the situation from our muscle tissues. Everything that we see, hear, feel, taste, and smell, which constitutes our "physical experience," our *sahu* takes literally and stores. The positive side of this can be seen for instance, in protecting us from a vicious dog. Upon approaching such an animal we are provided with the emotional response to either fight or flee, but, if we were traumatized by a dog at an early age. We would continue to fear and/or hate dogs based upon our childhood experience, and we may not even know why. The reason is because since our *sahu* does not possess the ability to make logical decisions. It cannot determine when we're in danger or not. To a person who has been traumatized by a dog, every time they see a dog – regardless of how big or small it is – their *sahu* would assume that they are in danger and release what it feels is the correct response.

When I compared this to how most people act and behave whenever they see spiders, mice and snakes, it made perfect sense. The scary truth I realized was that if we respond a certain way because our *sahu* is basically in the habit of doing so. Then, if our body breaks out in a rash, it would mean that it is our *sahu'* way of responding whenever we are irritated, feel that we are being ignored or not appreciated. If our body has an anxiety attack it could possibly be because we are worried about the near future and we're not sure how things will play out.

What this means is that everything that we have heard, smelled, tasted, touched (both the good and bad) is stored in *sahu*. All of these memories stored in our *sahu* influence the way we walk, talk, deal with others, etc. What is in our *sahu* therefore influences and shapes our ka (personality), khaibit (emotions/instincts) and khab (physical body), because it does not distinguish between right and wrong. It is simply responsible for helping us to survive by imitating anything and everything that we see. I believe that this is the reason why many religious founders claimed that we were born in sin. It is because our *sahu* not knowing right from wrong and imitating everything is simply ignorant about the nature of our Being. This again explains the reason why we have to be taught right from wrong, what is appropriate and inappropriate, etc. This also means that all living beings (plants and animals included) have a *sahu*.

The funny thing about our *sahu*, as I write this my daughter told my wife and I that my granddaughter who had just started pre-kindergarten school, amazed her teacher because she could already write her name and count to 20. Well, my granddaughter's teacher had started teaching her how to count to 25, so she would come home and count. But, when she stopped at 25, my daughter, trying to encourage my granddaughter to go to the next number, kept counting to 30. After several times of doing this my granddaughter angrily, told her mother,

"No, Mommy. There is no number after 25!"

Here my little beautiful, intelligent and naïve granddaughter shows the problem we all have with our *sahu*, because her teacher didn't teach her how to go beyond the number 25 yet. Never mind the fact that it was her mother that taught her how to count to 20 before she even met her teacher (proof of lack of reasoning). So, imagine how many of us cannot accomplish a particular feat because no one taught us how to go beyond what we **physical limitations**.

As you can see, we are a direct reflection of the paradigm that exists in our *sahu*. Whatever memories we have and dwell upon that exist in the lower division of the spirit, will affect our present. Good memories make us feel good because when our subconscious releases these memories they produce endorphins. Bad memories based upon traumatic events make us feel bad by releasing toxins into our body as a result.

Of course, no one in his or her right mind walks around angry and mad at the world all the time because no one wants to feel miserable all of his or her life[13]. We do however walk around thinking and focusing on events that have taken place in the past either to others or ourselves. When we think about negative events, all it does is make us more negative in our actions and behaviors unintentionally. If all you hear and think about is negativity that is the type of life you will have because the *sahu* accepts this as truth and produces the corresponding reaction. Despite our sincerest attempts to accomplish any goal, which means if you have a fear of losing money. It doesn't matter how much education you have, how many people you know, how much money you store away in your bank, etc. You will unintentionally lose your money through some strange circumstance. This is the reason most people that win the lottery shortly after lose all of their money and end up deeper in debt before they began.

I am not telling you this to spook you and make you believe that money is evil or the root of evil, which is absolute nonsense! This is a foolish, stupid and unwise remark that was made by someone that didn't understand how to make, manage and keep his or her own money. Because you have to have money in order to live, buy food, clothing and shelter. The purpose of telling you about our *sahu* is to make you aware. That it is superstitious, silly, outdated beliefs and ideas, which many of us learned from our parents that our subconscious is holding to. This is what is preventing most us from accomplishing our dreams by sabotaging our efforts with its emotions of pleasure and

---

[13] This is why it is advised to forgive your enemies but not forget what was done.

pain. But let's us not error and blame our parents for teaching us all of our wrong beliefs, because it is not totally our parents' fault. Our parents taught us the best they could. If our parents didn't know how to do a particular thing because no one taught them, how can we blame them for not teaching us something they didn't know? We can't because we are all victims and as Papa once told me, "We learn by our innocence," because this is life.

Accepting that this is how it is helped me to see that whenever I tried to break a habit and failed. It was not because I didn't have the will power to do so. Nor was it because my decision to break the habit was not a good one or vice versa. It was simply because my *sahu* was not motivated to help me towards my goal. To get our *sahu* to assist us in our goals we need heart – the ab.

Ab – The Spiritual Heart or Human Conscious

Fortunately, we are also given an *ab* that helps us the ability to reason. The *ab* is the part of our being that gives us the ability to observe, learn from our experience and make decisions based upon our conscience. It is our soul-self and although our *ab* may be influenced by the experiences and memories that have been stored in our *sahu*. It is not controlled by our *sahu*. At anytime, we can upon our choosing rise from the influences of our *sahu* and make a decisions for the improvement of our life, because God has given us the ability to be able control what influences our *sahu*, thus control our being. All we have to do is whatever we want our *sahu* to accept. We just need to intentionally, repetitiously and rhythmically impress what we want upon our *sahu*. This is how we learned our numbers and letters of the alphabets. It is funny to see that most of us when asked which letter comes first the letter "Q" or "P" we sing the "Alphabet Song" to get our *sahu* to release the memory.

It is our *ab* that makes man and woman different from all of the other beings on the planet, because it gives us the ability to ignore our *khabit* (animal instincts) that are under the influence of our *sahu*, and reason or "think". A fireman for instance, initial response when seeing a person in a burning building may be to flee the danger, but it is his *ab* that gives him the courage, strength and ability to quickly map out a route to save the individual. The same can be said about the mother upon hearing her child is in danger that will go through hell and back. These extraordinary acts are due to the *ab,* which provides us with courage, the ability to reason, and act based upon our conscience. This is the reason our *ab* is called our spiritual heart or conscience. It is because of our *ab* we bury our dead and wish them peace because our *ab* makes us believe that there is something that exists beyond death.

We are the only beings created by God that has an *ab,* but we are not born with our *ab* fully developed. We have to develop and strengthen our *ab* from birth because it is fragile and weak.

This is why we have to be taught how to reason, what is right from wrong and how to act courageously in the face of danger. Remember, it is our *sahu* that we have depended upon for most of our life because it is what helps us to survive. Our *sahu* is technically speaking is much older than our *ab* in regards to operation (at least by 14 years for most). We therefore have to develop and nurture our *ab,* which evolves based upon what we focus upon and our understanding. But, our *ab* relies a lot upon what exists in our *sahu.*

For this reason, a child should not be exposed to dangerous, disturbing, negative ideas, suggestions, thoughts and habits during her development years (when they are most receptive), because these negative influences will later reflect themselves in the child's intentional behavior as anger, anxiety, hostility, bad mannerisms, destructive social skills, etc. This is because their *sahu* has mimicked this behavior and now the child believes that this is the correct way to behave and do things. Children because their *ab* is not strong, but their *sahu* is fully functional are perfect mimickers like little parrots. So, if you cuss and use offensive language around your child, don't get angry with the child! They are only imitating what they have been exposed to because they do have not learned how to distinguish from appropriate and inappropriate behavior. Those of us who have parents from the southern States will now understand why when adults were speaking children were sent out of the room to play. It is because the conscious mind of the child has not been developed.

So we have to develop our *ab*, but here lies the problem. Since most of us were not raised in an environment that was full of knowledge, love, peace, wealth and prosperity. Most of us have some hang-ups because we had some undesirable experiences. Some of us had some bad parents, bad experiences with other people or animals. We have been in some rough situations and our *sahu* did the best it could to help us to survive to this day. But, it has also indiscriminately taken all of what we have experienced (the good and the bad) as truth. As a result, we have some pretty warped beliefs and ideas like money is the root of all evil, all women are evil, all men are dogs, etc., which is preventing us from enjoying life and fulfilling our destiny.

For instance, if you grew up in a household where your parents argued about money, worried about how the bills were going to be paid or you heard someone say "Money is the root of all evil". Your *sahu* recorded this experience and remembers it even if you can't recall it, so when you try to improve your finances. All of sudden you experience a loss and feel that something is not going to work. It is because you *sahu* remembers the previous experience and has assumed the worst. The experience that the *sahu* remembers, was made into a paradigm that we now live by, so whenever we decide to do anything. Automatically what come to mind are certain beliefs, ideas, thoughts and feelings. I like to use money as an example because it is the one thing that most people would like to have more. So, if I said most of us have within us a billion dollar idea just waiting to come out. If you didn't agree with this statement and had some skeptical thoughts that came into your awareness, those ideas that entered into your awareness are the ones that your *sahu* indiscriminately recorded about money.

Just imagine what else our *sahu* has stored that is preventing us from advancing and enjoying life. We have at least 14 years of good and bad memories that our *sahu* has recorded, because our *ab* did not begin to express itself until we were teenagers. And, if you can think about how inexperienced, immature, naïve and raw we were as teenagers. It should become clear that the reason our lives are not the

41

way we desire is because our ab has relied upon our sahu, which has created a paradigm based upon our limited physical experience.

The question that comes to mind then is how do we accomplish any goal if our *sahu* has retained some limited beliefs. Understand not everything that our *sahu* has learned is wrong. It is those things that we aren't happy with our life we can conclude is based upon a limited belief. Returning back to our subject, how do we accomplish a goal that we have no physical experience? How can a poor man become rich? How can an ill individual become healthy? It is by relying upon our *ba*.

The Ba – The Divine Conscious

The *ba* is division of our spirit based upon our unlimited inner-experience. It is the part of our being responsible for sending us hunches when we are in danger and giving us dreams. When you have you have an intuitive thought come to you, it was provided to you by your *ba*.

The *ba* has been called the collective unconscious; the super conscious, the Universal Mind and God because it is what connects us to all the living beings and has access to the storehouse of infinite information. But I do not believe it is God. I believe it is the divine spark that comes from God and connects us to the Divine. This in my opinion is the reason the Kamitic philosophers illustrated the *ba* as a human headed-falcon to signify that like the collective unconscious it is unlimited. The *ba* was symbolized as a falcon because falcons our trainable birds that will fly back to its owner, hence God. So it rests upon our head and when we retire, it is responsible for visiting places throughout the universe, which it communicates back to our *ab* and *sahu* as dreams.

Our ba is therefore, much stronger than our *sahu* because it is the direct opposite of our *sahu*. It draws from the Divine. You see, just like the purpose of the *sahu* is to help us to physically survive by providing us with a ka (personality), *khabit* (emotions/instincts) and

42

khab (physical body). The *ba* being the polar opposite is responsible for helping us to spiritually survive by providing us with *khu* (divine knowledge, spiritual wisdom), *shekhem* (divine instincts, spiritual power) and *ren* (spiritual name, destiny, or purpose). It is because of our *ba* that we feel that we have a higher calling and will get the urge to improve our wellbeing. It is because our *ba* is what connects us to the world beyond the physical and directly to God.

As mentioned earlier, when we are born it is our *sahu* that comes fully functioning in order to help us physically survive. Although our *ab* is undeveloped, our *ba* is fully functioning as well, which explains the reason why children our so open to spiritual beings (angels, ancestors and imaginary friends). The sad truth is that we all use to have a wonderful imagination when we were children and we believed that we could accomplish anything. So, what happened? Well, it was after living in the land of the living for 14 years or so, that we forgot that we were spiritual beings. We begin to identify more and more with our *sahu* (physical body conscious) and less with our *ba* (divine consciousness). As a result, most of us (myself included) only relied upon our *ba* and used it to pray to God when we were in desperate need. Why did we do this? Again, it is because this is what our *sahu* saw those around us do when they were in trouble and in need. Consequently, our *ba* faded into the background because we stop actively using it. Fortunately, it did not go away. It continues to hover above our head.

Since, the purpose of our *ba* is to help us to spiritually survive. The *ba* never completely leaves (If the *ba* completely leaves the body will cease to exist because it lacks purpose, which we will discuss in Chapter 6). All we need to do is to learn how to use it again like we did when we were children. The best way I have learned how to understand and use our *ba.* Like we did when we were children is by surrendering and accepting, that our *ba* has access to God, who knows and has power over everything. The reason we have to accept and surrender to our *ba* is because as soon as we begin to think about anything. It *sahu* will take the subject matter and try to figure out how to solve the problem based upon our limited physical experience. This prevents our *ba*, which is like a messenger bird from taking the problem to God.

43

That being said, the most important thing for parents to do with their children is to teach them how to remember and interpret their dreams, and practice concentrating until their *ab* is fully developed, so that when they reach adulthood they will have the ability to access their *ba* when they are older, thereby connect to the Divine.

So, when it is understood that our *sahu* takes everything literally (does not distinguish between right or wrong, real and unreal) and, accepts any command presented to it repetitiously as truth. Our *ab*, which gives us the ability to express our freedom, cannot control our *sahu*, but our *ba* can, because it has the divine power to help us to achieve whatever is humanly possible. The way to create positive change in our life is by choosing to put our *ab* in alignment with our *ba*, which will create a union with our *sahu*. In other words, we have to "trick" the *sahu* by making believing what we want, so that it can become a physical reality. This can be accomplished by taking symbols such as symbolic images, colors, gestures, music, metaphors, stories, etc., which our *sahu* is all fond of, and repetitiously using them so that our *sahu* will work with our *ba*.

Our job is to simply focus on what we want or hold a particular thought in our *ab* (heart), and let our *ba* and *sahu* do the rest, which is how we create habits. For instance, if a student wanted to improve their math scores, they would first make believe that they already have an "A" grade. This establishes in their *sahu* that they just need to maintain an "A" grade instead of trying to get something that they never had. Next, they would practice the correct way to do math problems until it became automatic, so when faced with a similar problem the *sahu* would unite with the *ba*, which would provide a solution on how to solve the problem.

If this method sounds familiar, it is because we have used it plenty of times in our life. Actors, athletes and musicians who all can attest that it has improved their performance presently use it. Speaking of musicians, it is known fact that some of the greatest entertainers before they became great practiced a 1,000 times in small clubs and in

44

front of small audiences before they became great performers. This is their secret to greatness.

This is what Kamitic spirituality is about. Instead of starting the race at the beginning, Kamitic philosophy teaches one to start the race at end by focusing upon what it is you want to achieve and working as if you have already achieved that goal (the end result). In other words, instead of assuming that you are in sin and trying to be holy, which our *sahu* has already established that it is impossible to live Christ-like. Kamitic philosophy begins by indicating that we were born Christ-like, we just have to learn how to maintain our holiness. This makes our *sahu* reasons is far easier to maintain something we already have then try to obtain.

We can all benefit from this technique because this is how all things came into existence. Everything that exists first came into existence from a belief, idea or thought. It was from this belief, idea or thought that emotions and feelings were created, which led to actions and later physical results. This means that all we have to do to achieve what we want out of life is to make the decision to do so and stick to it using our *ab*. This is harder than it seems, because remember, our *sahu* is much stronger than our *ab*. We have relied upon our *sahu* since birth so, it is much older than our *ab*, which we just began using when we were teenagers. This is the reason why when we tell our self that we are want to break a destructive habit like cigarette smoking, overeating, or create a constructive habit like exercising, we fail because we forget the process of making our dreams (beliefs, ideas and thoughts) a physical reality. We simply forget our divinity and forget that we have the ability to create the life we want like God.

So, to help remind us about our divinity, we will use the maa aankh to remind us that our *sahu* draws or learns from our limited physical experience of the Universe or TASETT. Our *ba* draws or learns from the unlimited spiritual experience of the Universe or KAMTA. And, our *ab*, which is free to choose do whatsoever we want is able to move between the two like the rising sun. Through the maa aankh we are able to see our self as a kingdom.

45

The Kingdom Within

"If a kingdom is divided against itself, it cannot stand."

Mark 3:24

By associating our sahu with TASETT and our ba with KAMTA, we can easily see that our limited knowledge is based upon our outer experience or physical-body conscious. (TASETT also symbolizes any physical or human institution, hence a type of Babylon).

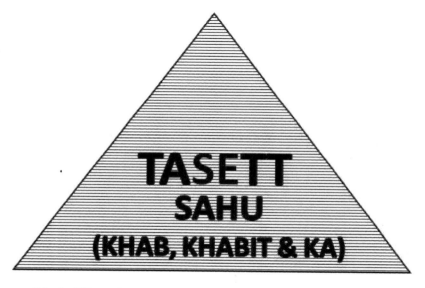

Limited Experience based upon our Physical-Body Experience
FIGURE 3: TASETT SYMBOLIZED AS THE SAHU

We easily see that divine conscious is unlimited because it is related to our understanding (actually inner-standing) or inner experience, KAMTA therefore symbolizes any spiritual institution, the realm of our ancestors and the higher state of mind. But, like Kamit, in order for us to prosper both our Lower and Upper Divisions of our Spirit must be united and must work together in harmony.

**Unlimited Experience based upon our Experience
with the Divine and all things Spiritual
FIGURE 4: KAMTA SYMBOLIZED AS THE BA**

Our ab is the ruler of both divisions. Just like the Two Great Lands of Kamit could only be united by one ruler. Our *ba* and *sahu* can only be united to work together through our *ab*. But our ab remember is not mature. It has to grow, evolve and be strengthened in order to express its true freedom and make wise choices and decisions. Our ab has to learn how to express its freedom by imitating God through the Khepera, Ra, Ra Atum and Amun Ra.

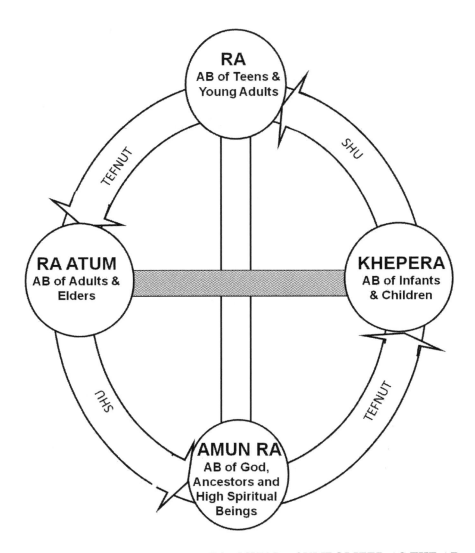

FIGURE 5: KHEPE-RA-RA ATUM AMUN RA SYMBOLIZED AS THE AB

We see that the ab of infants and children (symbolized as Khepera) is the polar opposite of the ab of adults and elders (symbolized as Ra Atum). The ab of youth, which is totally influenced by what was learned as child, is the polar opposite of the ab of God, the ancestors and other high spiritual beings such as angels. As you may have figured it out already, most people function from the Ra moment on the maa aankh, relying upon their physical senses and what they have learned as

48

children. Instead of learning how to develop and rely upon their Divine senses by moving their ab to the Amun Ra moment.

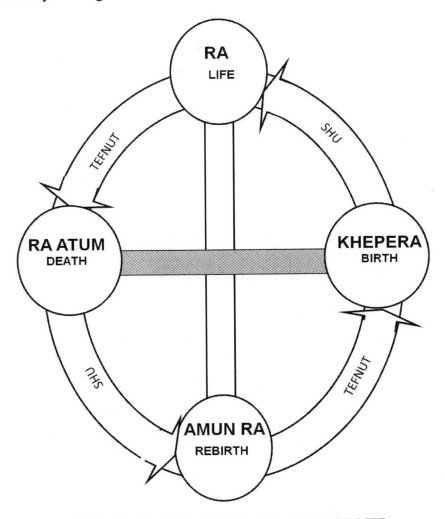

FIGURE 6: MAA AANKH AND THE CYCLE OF LIFE

The Amun Ra moment as you can see relates to our understanding or inner-standing (intuitive faculties). From a psychological perspective our *ab* evolves based upon observations. It mirrors the movement of the sun. It goes through the entire cycle of being born and living. Then our ab metaphorically dies due to erroneous beliefs, ideas and thoughts,

49

etc. that we have learned earlier in life. The only way for our *ab* to be reborn is by learning from our past mistakes and replacing incorrect beliefs, ideas and thoughts, with spiritual truths. This can only be accomplished through Divine/Spiritual means.

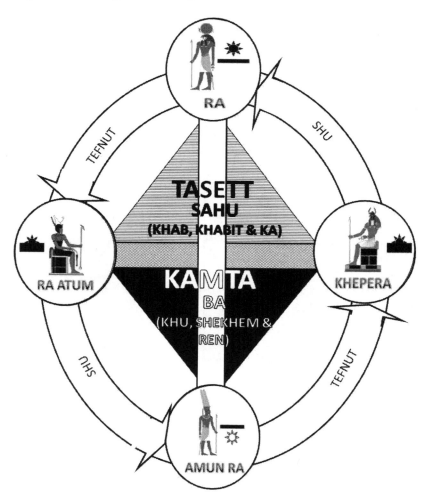

**FIGURE 7: DIVISIONS OF THE SPIRIT
SYMBOLIZED AS THE MAA AANKH**

Through the maa aankh, we are reminded of our uniqueness amongst all beings and our divinity by seeing that we are a microcosm of the Greater Macrocosm. Since there is no other being like us that exist,

50

because we are the only living beings that were created and given a free will because we were created in the image of God. Logically in order to succeed in life, we have to choose God as our role model and learn how to unite our kingdom within.

Study Questions

1. What is the Spirit?
   The Spirit is called the Rau in the Kamitic language and it manifests itself metaphysically and physically throughout the Universe.

2. What is the sahu?
   The sahu is the Lower Division of the Rau that corresponds to our subconscious mind, which controls all of our autonomous body functions and stores our personal memories, experiences and genetic memories.

3. What is the *sahu* responsible for and what does the *sahu* provide?
   The *sahu* is responsible for helping us to physically survive. The *sahu* provides us with our *khab* (physical body), the *khabit* (our emotions and animal instincts), and a *ka* (our personality).

4. What is the *ab*?
   The *ab* is the part of our being that gives us the ability to learn from observation and the freedom to make conscious and rational decisions. It is called the *ab* because is corresponds to our spiritual heart (conscience), conscious and courage.

5. How does the *ab* evolve?
   The *ab*, which is always aware, evolves based upon what we focus upon and our understanding. When we surrender our *ab* to our *ba*, this is when we are able to acquire wisdom and thereby see the consequences of our actions, which results in evolution.

51

6. What is *ba* and is it God?

   The *ba* is the higher division of the spirit that corresponds to our unconscious mind, collective unconscious, the universal mind, the super conscious, etc. It is responsible for helping us to spiritually survive by providing us with *khu* (divine knowledge, spiritual wisdom), *shekhem* (divine instincts, spiritual power) and *ren* (spiritual name, destiny, or purpose). The *ba* is not God. It is the divine spark that belongs to God symbolized as a human-falcon because it delivers our requests to God and communicates back to our *ab* and *sahu* through our dreams.

7. Briefly, explain how Khepera, Ra, Ra Atum and Amun Ra correspond to our *ab*.

   Khepera symbolizes our *ab* in its beginning evolutionary stage when we are children. Ra is the moment our *ab* has evolved to the point   that we can express our freedom and make choices based upon what we have learned, which many times may not be correct.

   Ra Atum represents the decisions we have made that have led us to see that something is not correct. It is here we see what we have learned is not correct, so we naturally look for ways to make changes. Amun Ra is the moment we begin to make changes in our life through divine intervention (hunches, inspiring ideas, etc.). It is the moment we meet the Divine.

8. What happens when you move your *ab* to the Amun Ra point?

   When you move your *ab* to the Amun Ra point your awareness is shifted to the metaphysical or spiritual aspects of the Spirit that exist in the Universe.

9. How do you effectively make changes to the TASETT?

   By repetitively using symbols such as symbolic images, colors, gestures, music, metaphors, stories and thoughts, so that the TASETT unites with KAMTA.

10. Jesus said, "If a kingdom is divided against itself, it cannot stand." (Mark 3:24). What does this scripture mean in regards to the maa aankh?

It means that we need our *sahu* to work with our *ba* or our TASETT and KAMTA to unite as one, because our *ab* or our suns cannot do it alone.

Exercise: How to Talk and Listen to God

KAMTA is our place of refuge. It our place of rest and where we can find the solution to any problem we face. We can enter into KAMTA at anytime and anywhere by simply holding a thought, idea, symbol, etc. in mind. Two of the easiest ways we can enter into KAMTA is through prayer and meditation.

Praying and meditating does not have to be difficult. The problem that most people have with praying and meditation is that they don't understand that both are simply forms of communicating to God. It is because of this misunderstanding, most people usually don't pray unless it is their last resort, and when they do simply repeat a set of meaningless words. Their prayer has no conviction and no sustenance because we they entered into prayer they have doubts, fears and worries on their mind. The prayer ends up coming out of their mouth as:

> *Oh heavenly Father. I your humble, dragged and*
> *undeserving servant ask can you please bless me*
> *with some change, bread and water. I would be*
> *ever so grateful for whatever you give me. Thank*
> *you...Sir?*

This is not a prayer! This is a plea from a beggar! What comes to my mind is Charles Dickens's fictional character and story of the same name *Olive Twist*. Olive Twist remember was a thief, which means when we pray like this, we feel automatically that we are not going to get what we want anyway, so it is part of a ploy to steal it. This is not the correct way to pray. If you remember what was said about the *sahu*. If you want something, you have to enter into prayer with complete conviction.

53

You have to pray to God or talk to God like God is right in front of you and is your closest friend. You have to dispense with the "niceties" and just talk with the knowing and understanding. That there is only One Supreme Being, who knows all, sees all and is everywhere. That will provide us with everything we need and want, at the right time, in the right space and sequence. At the same time, we have to understand that communication is a two-way street. If we talk, we have to be willing to listen. The listening part of praying is meditation.

Prayer

The easiest prayer that you can say is by expressing your gratitude simply by saying, "Thank you" for everything that you are pleased with in your life.

By saying, "Thank you" for everything that you are grateful for, you are creating a thought through your *ab* that will generate an emotional feeling of happiness in your *sahu*, which will unite with the *ba* and inspire more blessings. From a spiritual perspective this means that God upon seeing that you are grateful for what you have will then send you more blessings along the same line. If you express gratitude for food, friendship, etc. then you will continue to receive food, friendship, etc. It may not make sense but try it for your self and see if it works.

Once you have experienced joy from expressing your gratitude. You may either continue saying this same simple prayer or use some of the more popular prayers that exist to express your authority like the Lord's Prayer or Twenty-Third Psalms. Avoid prayers that are expressed as wimpy pleas for help and make you feel like you are a weak and have no control in your life. These types of prayer will not only make you feel like you are weak, helpless, but also that if God chooses to save you it is because God pities you. It is not a matter of God choosing to help you or not. It is a matter of believing that you deserve to be helped.

You must understand that it is in God's best interest to make you prosperous, successful, and healthy, etc. because it only glorifies God and makes you a stronger surrogate or vessel. So, don't pity yourself. Reject all forms of negative self-talk and learn how to talk to God.

Meditation

The easiest way to meditate is to simply relax your body and let go of all the tension in your muscles. Simply allow your mind to run free by ignoring all the ideas and thoughts that come to your awareness. Try not to think about anything that comes to mind. Just relax and let all of the ideas and thoughts that come to your awareness just pass through. Practice this exercise every day until you are able to enter into the state awareness with ease.

The more you relax and focus on achieving this state of awareness throughout life, the easier it will become for you to identify with true nature of your being Amun Ra. The more you practice this exercise. The more relax you will become and slower to anger you will become as well. You will also find that eventually others will not be able to easily influence you with their ideas, thoughts and beliefs.

When you use this meditative technique along with prayer, you will receive inspirational ideas that will come to you through visions, dreams, occurrence and hunches, etc. That will help make your life a lot easier. All you have to do is learn to trust in the responses being given to you. Through practice it will become easier for you to distinguish between these responses coming from KAMTA and the various influences coming from TASETT. In time, you will learn that the inspiration coming to your awareness will not lead you astray or tell you something that you are not prepared to handle. It will not inform you to do something out of character nor make life more difficult for you. It is solely concerned with helping you to reach your potential and obtain peace in your life.

55

Always remember that you can talk to God anywhere (home, car, at the park, on the beach, etc.). So, when you receive a new idea that comes to your awareness to express your gratitude by simply saying, "Thank you."

CHAPTER 4

How to Get Power through Your Intuition

*All is within yourself. Know your most inward self and look for what corresponds
with it in nature.*

Kamitic Proverb

As we have read previously, our *sahu* consists of our limitations but
our *ba* is unlimited, which means we can change our life the way we
want by initiating change through our *ba*. If you think of KAMTA as
being dark fertile soil, a womb, the night sky, etc. that is full of
potential, all that is required is that we learn how to sow seed or our
desire, so that it manifests itself physically. This is how we change our
paradigm and one of the ways to accomplish this is by using our
intuition.

Before we begin, so that we are all on the same page, let me
explain what I mean when I say using our intuition. Intuition means
obtaining information by using our inner sense of sight, hearing, smell,
taste, and touch. It is an inner knowing and although the word is
commonly used interchangeably with clairvoyance and telepathy. It is
different in the sense of how the information is given and received,
whereas telepathy deals with sending information and clairvoyance
deals with transferring information that is unknown to an individual.

For instance, have you ever thought about a person and
suddenly you ran into that individual or got a phone call from them.
The reason you became aware of that individual or thing or vice versa,
are because everything that exists has the ability to create a signal
because it has a lower spirit. That signal (our thought or idea) is
transferred to the *ba* and received through our *ka* (referred to as our
double), which is a division in our *sahu* that acts as antennae.

To create change using our intuition, we use this ability to see past events and how those events effect the present. But we cannot see is the future because the future has not been written. This is the reason why most psychics and prophesiers can for the most part tell you with an uncanny accuracy. About things going on in the past and events revolving around you presently, but when it comes to the future they are almost always dead wrong. It is because KAMTA is not restricted by time, which means the future has not been determined yet. Since KAMTA is not restricted by time, no one knows what tomorrow will bring because it has not been written. This means the future is not determined by what was done in the past but what is done today in the present.

I learned this the hard way. As I mentioned earlier, I was told by prophesiers that I was supposed to be a preacher, but the thing that use to always get me. Was that these people could never tell me anything exact such as how to go about being a preacher, so this contributed to my disgust about my calling. It also made me develop a bad taste in my mouth about people that prophesized. Over the years, after hearing the same "prophecy" so many times but not given a road map on how to become a preacher or learn my destiny. It became old and useless news, more like a gimmick, still the subject seem to fascinate me as I became older.

It wasn't until some years later, that I met young man who had the gift of sight. That made some pretty good predictions that would come true. At the time, I was quite desperate because I was homeless, unemployed and didn't have any money at all. So, I decided to get a reading from this young man in order to get a hint as to what I was supposed to do or at least how to get some money. This along with the fact that he was going to give me the reading free of charge, made me put aside my prejudices, and gives it a try.

At the start of the reading just like it was in B-thriller movies, I was told about the things that had happened in my past. Next, I was told about the things going on in my life in the present. Then, when it came to my future, he gave me some very vague instructions because he said he couldn't see that far ahead. He told me a man is going to ask me to do something and informed me not to do it. What man? He didn't know. How did the man look? He didn't know. When was the man going to ask me to do something? He didn't know. Who was the man? You guessed it. He didn't know. Just a man... Now, like I said, I was a guest in this young man's mother's house so, when his older brother asked me to get the door because someone was knocking at it. How could I refuse? This is the logical conclusion that the psychic picked up on, that obviously living in another person's house I was going to answer the door when asked to do so. At the door were robbers who came in with a double barrel shotgun. Again, how was I supposed to know that this 18-year-old kid was the man that the psychic was talking about in the reading?

The difference between intuition and psychic ability as you can see is the former deals with an inner knowing, whereas the latter depends upon speculation. When people claim to see the future they are actually just picking up on the possibilities, which you don't have to be a psychic to do. This is what the young man who gave me a reading did. Most news programs make predictions all of the time. This is the reason why you cannot worry about what might happen, because the future is dependent upon what occurs in the present.

By developing and working with your intuition, you for the most part go by what you can sense connected around you. When you move your *ab* to the Amun Ra point you are able to pick up on other peoples' perceptions and situations by simply tuning into their frequency, because of the dialogue between the *ba* and *sahu*. Remember, if your *ab* is hovering over the TASETT at the Ra moment you would not be able to pick up on other peoples' perceptions. You like most people would go about your normal day exchanging and receiving thoughts from others but thinking that these thoughts originated from your own mind. It is only because you moved your *ab* to the Amun Ra moment that you are able to focus or tune into the vibes of others and everything around you. When you move your *ab* to the Amun Ra moment under KAMTA, the *ba* through the *khu*, takes into account all of the factors that exist in the TASETT (gravity, the individual, who the individual is around, the environment, etc.) in order to obtain the information you desire. This is how the *ba* and *sahu* work together like KAMTA and TASETT. One of the easiest ways I have found how to understand how to work with your intuition is through the use of oracles.

Oracles are tools used to communicate with the Divine and other spiritual beings. People from various backgrounds have used them all over the world. There is even considerable mention of oracles used throughout the bible. For instance, in Genesis 44:4-5 and 15, Joseph the Dreamer who was considered to be the wisest man in ancient Egypt according to biblical lore, is found to possess a divination vessel that was used to allow one to obtain messages through symbols seen in liquids. He used this form of divination, a common Kamitic technique called scrying, to interpret dreams in Genesis Chapter 40 and 41, because God according to scripture speaks to human beings through their dreams.

Besides scrying and interpreting dreams there are other forms of divination that are mentioned in the bible as well. Throughout the Old Testament there is mentioned that certain priests had an Urim and Thummim. These are oracles which in Leviticus 16:7-8, the priest used to understand the will of God, which answered yes and no questions according to Deuteronomy 33:8. In Numbers 27:2, Ezra 2:62-63, and Nehemiah 7:64-65, one can find further use of this oracle. There is also mention of the use of an oracle in the New Testament as well. In Acts 1:24-26, the eleven apostles cast lots to find a replacement for Judas. The reason these oracles were used is because it was believed that God did not talk directly to human beings like he did with Abraham, Moses or Jesus. Instead God used signs to communicate His will.

Now, I learned two valuable lessons from that experience with the robbers. The first was that our intuition is a great guide to have because it can definitively protect us from danger. The second lesson was that it does you no good just to follow a hunch just because you got a stroke of inspiration. Some good ole logical reasoning should always support your intuition.

I say this because as I mentioned before. I was told several times I was supposed to be a preacher when I was younger, but if I had listened to some of these people and just got on the bandwagon to go into the pulpit. Who knows what would have happened without proper knowledge, wisdom and experience. Thankfully, I waited and I know now that God does not reveal something to you that you aren't prepared to deal with. God knows what you know and what you are ready for. God knows your past and your future. God would never put you in a situation that you are not prepared to address. I have learned that when it is meant for you to do something, a path will be laid before you to take. I have on numerous occasions wanted or needed some help in a particular area of interests and when I stopped stressing about it. I was led to the answer, the solution or to someone who could help me. So let's be clear. God is not going to reveal to you how to do open heart surgery if you don't know anything about how the heart functions. An excellent example of this can be seen in the HBO film *Something The Lord Made*, which is about the black cardiac pioneer Vivien Thomas, who in the movie after doing postdoctoral cardiac research. Had a dream, which contributed to Dr. Alfred Blalock procedure for treating blue baby syndrome.

For this reason, there are three important points that I found one should always keep in mind while developing your intuition and using oracles. The first and most important is that oracles do not and will not tell you what to do. We were given mind so that we can choose to do whatever we want. So any question that begins with "Should I do this or that?" will appear to be an ambiguous question. The response to such a question will yield a doubtful and uncertain answer. If there is something you want to know. Then ask and allow your *ba* to reveal it to you. You may also want to avoid asking "test" questions.

The second point to remember is that the key to interpreting any oracle is being able to understand the signs or meaning of the symbols. This means that both your *sahu* and *ba* have to be working together. If for instance, you are not focusing on the stock market and you received information on buying stocks that will make you rich. This 99.99% of the time is not coming from your *ba* but your *sahu*. Knowing this has helped me out tremendously. As a result, I know that when I am focusing on something but for whatever reason I don't get the message because I am too tired, not meditating, whatever. The message comes

61

to me in other ways usually through a conversation with someone, while watching television, hearing a message on the radio, etc. I have had complete strangers come up to me and tell me something I needed to hear and later disappear out of my life. It is all because my *ba* is speaking through them.

The third point is to always offer a word of thanks for the information you have received.

Always remember, the answer you receive from any oracle is simply telling you about what resides in your *sahu*. It is revealing to you what you may not want to hear but need to, that sometimes has nothing to do with the situation you asked about. Again, this is a conversation between you and the Divine, and God does not lie. So, if ever you receive an answer that comes to you intuitively that you know is correct, but you don't like. Resist the urge to ask, deny and ignore what was revealed to you.

If you do happen to receive an answer that you do not like, then yell at your *sahu*. Tell your sahu what you want now! This forceful gesture and response will make a strong impression upon your *sahu* and influence it to work favorably with your *ba* in yielding better results.

The Divining Art of Bibliomancy

One of most commonly used forms of divination used by preachers and ministers is called bibliomancy. I learned about this method after watching my father and other preachers prepare to deliver a sermon. The basic process that many of them use is to get into a contemplative mindset by first praying or talking to God. Next they ask what is that they need to preach or tell the congregation. Then they focus intently on question and allow their *ba* and *sahu* to direct their attention. Through this divination method their attention is guided to a particular passage in the bible, which becomes the theme of the sermon. But bibliomancy does not have to be used with the bible. It can be used with any book. All you have to do is ask the question. Focus upon it and ask to be shown the solution to the problem you seek. Next, allow your intuition to guide you to the book that will answer your question. Note the images and impressions come to your awareness.

The key to using this form of divination effectively is having an understanding of the medium you are using. When I first learned about the maa aankh, this information was given to me through bibliomancy, because I had read and studied the Kamitic history for so many years. It basically became a suitable medium for me to receive insight.

Any fable, legend, myth, or story rich in symbolism, studied and contemplated upon for a long time. Will appear so entertaining to our *sahu* that is will by-pass it, thus allowing our *ba* to provide us with deep, flashes of insight, which could not be expressed in words. After receiving this insight, be sure to express your gratitude by saying, "Thank you."

Using Natural Signs as an Oracle

Just like verbal symbols (fables, legends, myths and stories) can provide flashes of insight. Visual symbols when contemplated upon have the ability to do the same thing. We all symbols that are precious to us and we also have symbols that we share. The color red for instance is an example of a symbol that we all share because the very mention of it makes us think, "Stop, danger, hot, fire, caution, etc." An owl is an example of a symbol that may be precious to us. For some people the owl symbolizes wisdom but for others, it may symbolize death, but which one is right? Neither because it all pertains to the understanding of the individual and what the symbol means to that individual.

Let me give you an example. I use to believe that owls symbolized wisdom, but when I met my wife and learned that owls to her symbolized death. My understanding of this symbol changed and I began to see owls as symbol of wisdom, but if one did not heed to the wise ways it would lead eventually to death.

So, learn how to appreciate and interpret what symbols mean to you. The easiest way to do is by studying the symbols found in nature. Since every place in nature radiates a certain type of energy and when you develop your intuition, you can pick up on these influences and use them to initiate change. By studying nature especially the behaviors of animals, it will become easier for you to interpret how events will play out.

Another way to use natural signs is based upon the *maa* and is an exchange of energy. Since what goes up must come down, what goes in must come out, etc. With this method you ask your question such as "How do I do this?" Then even though you do not have the answer for the question but have faith that you will receive an answer. You offer a glass of water, a piece of fruit, a candle of your choice, incense, coins, money, etc. (whatever you feel to give). This simple gesture implies that you have faith in God that your request will be answered. It also sends energy into your *ba*, which will return its way back to you because the energy in KAMTA flows northward towards TASETT. Again, be sure to express your gratitude once your objective is achieved.

The Fishing Net Oracle

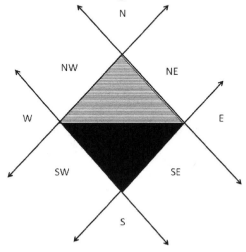

Another very simple oracle that I have found to be very useful especially for quick answers such as predicting how events will unfold is what I call the Fishing Net oracle, named as such because of its pattern. It consists of drawing a diagonal tic-tac-toe pattern to create a diamond in the center to symbolize the unified KAMTA and TASETT. The surrounding eight spaces represent the eight directions.

To use this oracle, you enter into a meditative state of mind and then take a cowry shell (a white pebble, a small white quartz stone, a white bean, etc.) to symbolize your pure intentions, and tell it what you would like to know. Then drop the shell and record where it falls. Below are general interpretations of the shell placement:

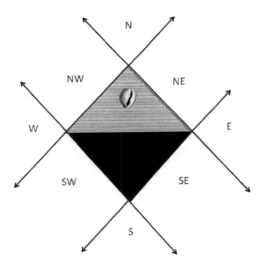

Diamond: If the shell falls in the center it indicates that your *ba* and *sahu* are working together for a common goal. Note that if it falls in the TASETT portion, it indicates that things will happen very quickly. If it falls in the KAMTA field, then the creative forces are being moved towards the physical manifestation of your objective. If the question was about an upcoming trip, the voyage will be successful but a blessing should be conducted for extra protection. If the question is about an illness, the individual most likely came in contact with an infected garment contaminated with negative energy. A blessing ritual for health may be helpful for full recovery.

East: A very good sign symbolizing prosperity and success in all endeavors. If illness is present it is due to contact with an envious aapepu, which will be discussed in the next chapter. The necessary action is needed to drive this aapepu away.

Northeast: This is a very good sign. It marks the beginning of a new beginning, new life and abundance. Expect good news and a blessing of peace.

North: Danger, conflict, obstacles, loss and illness. Anything lost will be difficult to recover.

Northwest: An okay sign that is neither good nor bad. It implies that energy is leaving and setting in the west. If the question is about illness, it will not go away anytime soon. If you have visitors they will bring problems into your life.

West: The direction of harvest is a very good sign for personal affairs but not for group efforts. If illness is present it is due to contact with an aapepu.

Southwest: A very ominous sign symbolizing bad luck, deprivation, loss, misfortune, etc. It is time for a serious change.

South: Being near Amun Ra point makes this a good sign. It indicates that anything that has been lost will soon be recovered. Illness and misfortunes are the result of an imbalance due to an offense to one's ancestors and guardian spirits. Express your gratitude for what you have and perform a blessing ritual to restore balance.

Southeast: A good omen indicating rebirth and return of all that is good. If there is illness that is present it will soon go away.

This is just a couple of ways to develop your intuition. Feel free to explore your own and learn how to become comfortable with your symbols.

Study Questions

1. What does intuition mean?
   Intuition means obtaining information by using our inner sense of sight, hearing, smell, taste, and touch.

2. What can our intuition be used for?
   We can use our intuition to see past events and how those events effect the present.

3. Can you see into the future using your intuition? If not why?
   No you cannot see into the future using your intution because the future has not been written yet.

4. Why is it impossible to see into the future?
   It is impossible to see into the future because KAMTA is unlimited and there are numerous choices available.

5. What is the division of our spirit under our *ba* that allows us to intuit called?
   The division of the spirit that allows us to intuit is called the khu.

6. Can oracles tell you what to do?
   No oracles can only reveal to you possible solutions to a problem. Only we have the *ab* to do what we want.

7. How do oracles work?
   Oracles work by creating a bridge between our *ba* and *sahu*.

8. If your ab is hovering over the TASETT at the Ra moment can you pick up on other people's perceptions?
   If your *ab* is hovering over the TASETT at the Ra moment you would not be able to pick up on other peoples' perceptions. You like most people would go about your normal day exchanging and receiving thoughts from others but thinking that these thoughts originated from your own mind

9. What happens when you move you ab to the Amun Ra moment?

When you move your *ab* to the Amun Ra point you are able to pick up on other peoples' perceptions and situations by simply tuning into their frequency, because of the dialogue between the *ba* and *sahu*

10. When people claim to be able to see the future. What are they picking up on?

They are picking up on the possibilites or the "ifs" that could happen that exist in our *sahu*.

Exercise: How to Develop Your Intuition

There are several ways to develop one's intuition to create change but one of the easiest and simplest methods I have found is by trying to achieve a goal.

Many times the reason people are not happy with their lives because they do not know what they want. Remember, KAMTA is a big place that has no beginning or end, so if you do know what you want or where you are going. You are bound to end up with anything and anywhere.

Ask yourself what is that you want? Take time and really develop your answer so that you know exactly what it is that you want. Do not worry about how you will achieve the goal or get what you want at this moment. Just focus for right now on what it is that you want. By asking yourself this question you will begin to focus and direct your *sahu* and *ba* towards a common goal. This procedure will also force you to ask yourself if what you want is worth your time and energy.

Next, picture in your mind exactly what it is that you want. Do not focus on the steps or concern yourself with how your goal will be accomplished. Simply imagine the end result, such as how you will feel when you have achieved your goal. Try imagining how others will feel when you have accomplished your goal. Ask yourself what problems will you have solved when you have achieved your goal. Try as best you can to understand the feelings that you would have once your goal has come to pass.

When you have imagined your goal as much as possible, to the point that mere mention or thought of it conjures up the emotions you will have, when the goal has been achieved. Write down how you would feel once your goal has been accomplished and how it makes others feel. Then, write down how you think you would go about achieving your goal. Try to be as clear and concise as possible. By doing this you will notice that there are numerous ways that you can accomplish your goal. If there are ways that enter your awareness that you are not comfortable with write those down as well and explain why you would not take this route. Continue focusing upon how you would go about achieving your goal and write those options down.

Once you have written all of your choices down. Narrow your choices down to the one way you would choose to accomplish your goal. Only choose the option that feels like the right one that will lead you to accomplishing or achieving what you want. Make sure that you can honestly say to yourself, "I believe, this course of action will lead me to my goal." When you can say this, write this down course of action down.

Now take what you have written down and put it away inside of a box, a drawer or wherever for a few days, and try not to think about the results at all. This may be hard not to think about how you are going to achieve your goal, but do the best you can. This is not to say that you should not imagine how you would feel when you have accomplished your goal. You simply should try not to think about how to achieve your goal. If at any time you find yourself thinking about what you have written down. Simply recognize it for what it is and permit it to pass out of your awareness. This forces your *sahu* to hand over the project to your *ba*.

After a few days have passed, take the paper out and review it to see if you still feel the same way about your goal. And, if you still want to follow the chosen course to achieving what you want. You may find that you might want to change some things or go about doing something in another way. Many times when I have used this method to get something I wanted. A new and easier route appears that I didn't even consider. Some times after reviewing all of my choices it is revealed to me that I am not ready for what I want, which is the reason why all my efforts to get what I want have failed.

The reason you are encouraged not to think about how to achieve your goal, is because your *ba* may present you with a route that you many never have considered. For instance, before I learned how to engage my *ba*. One day I applied for a new job because at the present job I was at I really felt like I was unappreciated. This new job I had applied for I had no idea how to do it but I felt confident in my abilities. I was denied the job, but it didn't stop me from applying again. Months went by and I didn't hear anything about the job I had applied for but I really wanted to quit my present job. Again, I was denied the job.

When, I learned about how to work my *ba*. I wrote down that I wanted a new job because I was miserable at my present job and wanted more money. Naturally, I wrote down that the only way to get what I wanted was to get a new job by searching the classifieds. I put the paper up and for a few days. I didn't think or obsess about getting a new job at all. I completely allowed my *ba* to work on it. Several days later, I got a hunch to look on the Internet and I found a job posting for a different position with the same company I had applied for previously. I applied and sure enough I got the job, which paid more than what I was making at my current job for less amount of time. After being on the job for a year in a half, I was offered the job I had previously applied for in the beginning. Some might call it a miracle; say that it was magic or that I was in the right place at the right time. But, when you know how to work with the power of God, it is simply a matter of faith.

70

CHAPTER 5

How to Get Power through Dreaming

Listen to your conviction, even if they seem absurd to your reason.

Kamitic Proverb

Have you ever had a dream that felt so real that you had to check yourself to see if it was or not? How do you know it was a dream or a reality? For that matter how do you know that right now you aren't dreaming while reading this book?

It is our *ab* that determines what is real and not real and therefore it determines who we are and what we will be. Not our *ba* or *sahu*. This is very important to understand a lot of people are not happy with their lives because they are living in the past. They have had this experience and that traumatic experience, and now they believe they can't do anything to change it. This is totally untrue. For example, there are many that believe that because they were born in poverty that they shall always live in poverty. Even though there are numerous examples found throughout history of people in similar situations and worst that have become wealthy. When we keep the maa aankh firmly in mind, we see that anything is possible so long as we believe and one of the ways of creating change is through dreaming.

Before we begin, it must be remembered that our universe according to the maa aankh is divided into KAMTA and TASETT. TASETT is the outer world and is the symbol for outer expression. When we are born, it is our *sahu* that comes functioning intact so that we can immediately learn from our physical or outer experience. This is the reason the Kamitic word for the physical, outer experience, physical objects, the earth and any celestial body/planet is called a seb or sba. Variations of the same word were used for education, training, instructions, etc., while an instructor, teacher and trainer were called sbai and variations of the word sba refers to morning or daytime. These are all reference that the outer world and daytime were seen as symbols of the physical realm.

KAMTA corresponds to the inner world, because KAMTA is the Black Lands, it also refers to that which is unseen, hidden, and the night. It was called for this reason the Underworld or the *Tuat "12 Hours of Night", Amenta "The Hidden Land* or *Land of Amun"* (see the maa aankh) and so on. This is because this is where God, the angels, ancestors, spirit guides, guardian spirits and all of the mysterious spiritual beings exist and reside. This is why sunset was called Ra Atum *"The Completed Ra"* because it marked the beginning of a new day. Sunrise was referred to as *Khepera "The Ra Coming Into Being"* because it is the moment that physical things from out of the mysterious night come into existence.

It is this understanding that has led me to believe that because the word *"khem"* or *"kam"* means black in the Kamitic language. That when the Kamitic people called themselves Kamau, which translates to mean "Black People". They were not just referring to the color of their skin and ethnicity. While I understand the cultural and historical importance of classifying the Kamitic people as being of African descent in our color conscious world that refuses to acknowledge contributions made by African people. I believe that the Kamitic people called themselves Kamau to express the importance they placed on the spiritual realm, and indicate that they came from the mysterious land of the Spirit. This corresponds with other traditional African philosophy like the Yoruba who say that *"The world is a marketplace, the otherworld is our home."* The significance of this is to point out that we are born onto the earth or in the physical realm in order to learn a specific lesson. In other words, we are in the physical world just to visit and experience the outer reality. Our real home is KAMTA where we are able to create changes to our physical reality through dreaming.

If you can imagine KAMTA being the night sky, a sacred grove, the mysterious deep, the cemetery, the forest, a jungle or bush that the slaves escaped to meet with God, etc. It should come to no surprise that the deeper you go into it. The more difficult it is to maintain your focus because KAMTA is a big place and easy to get lost. This is why those new to meditation and prayer will often find that their focus will wander. I remember because I didn't know how to pray I would usually start praying on my knees and wake up with a crook in my neck because I fell asleep lying between the floor and my bed. When I first learned how to meditate, I would fall asleep after taking a few deep breaths. It was because KAMTA is deep and very mythical. Venturing into KAMTA is like taking a road trip across the country without a map. It is like running in dark with no flashlight and so on.

So spiritual practitioners from all over the world created spiritual roadmaps to help people in their travels across KAMTA or said another way. To help people move their *ab* from the Ra Atum moment and to the Khepera. All of the great funerary texts like the Kamitic *Pert em Hru (Egyptian Book of the Dead)* and the Tibetan *Bardol Thodol* (the so-called Tibetan *Book of the Dead*) are in truth mythical writing describing how to go deeper into KAMTA. In these texts the initiated dreamer is instructed to greet, offer, say, motion, and become a specific resident in the otherworld, because KAMTA is unlimited and has to be given conscious intent on what to do. Does it make sense now why we were created? We were created to be God's eyes, ears, hands, mouth, etc. We were created to come into the world of the living, survey it and report back to God what was going on. If there is a problem, while our awareness is in KAMTA we acquire a solution so that we can come back and implement the physical change in TASETT.

As you can see, the so-called hierarchy that is said to exist in the inner world (or heavens) is a label that human beings created to order our thinking and understanding, but in truth there is no hierarchy per such because KAMTA is unstructured. How else could you close your eyes you only see darkness. So, the funerary texts that were written were created to help people to function in their dreams, because if you can control your dreams, you can influence your physical reality.

It should become clear now that most of the religious texts that have been written, including myths, legends and fables, are actually records of an individual's dream between them (the dreamer) and the

Divine. Just think about the various stories and myths where the Divine reveals itself to the pious. To the laymen or the outsider (hence *sahu* - TASETT the outer expression), upon hearing the story it would be interpreted as being literal because our rational logical mind would not be able to comprehend the experience. This is the reason Ra reveals his secret name to Oset in secret and, why the Lord tells Moses to warn the people not to gaze upon Him or they would perish.

There are several types of dreams that can be used to create change in our physical reality. There are prophetic dreams; revelation dreams that reveal life-changing messages and teaching dreams that help us to spiritually grow. In Our *Dreaming Mind* author Robert Van De Castle cites that the escaped slave, Harriet Tubman who led hundreds of slaves to freedom through the "Underground Railroad" would have dreams that helped her to find safe passageways. There are inspirational dreams such as the dream that Martin L. King Jr. inspired people from diverse groups to create a colorblind society. Below are the most common dreaming techniques and ways of how they can be used to improve the quality of your life.

Night Dreaming

Everyone and every living thing that exist night dreams, because if you didn't you would not be alive today. This why even animals have dreams, of course no one knows exactly what a dog is dreaming of when they bark in their sleep. Maybe they are chasing a cat or defending their bones, but every living thing has night dreams because everything has a *sahu* and a *ba*. The difference between human beings and all of the other living beings on the planet is that we have an *ab*, which gives us the ability to express our will freely. It is because of our *ab* we can choose to change our dreams. But before we can change our night dreams we have to learn how to recall and interpret them.

Recalling Night Dreams

The simplest way to recall your night dreams is to keep a dream journal. You do not need anything fancy. All you need is to keep a writing pad near your nightstand or by your bed. When you awake after having a dream simply rewrite the dream as your remember it. Try to write down every detail as strange as it may seem. Do not focus on interpreting and understanding the dream for now. Just relax and write the dream down. The more you get into the habit of writing your dreams. The easier it will become for you to recall your night dreams and soon you will begin to notice how your everyday affairs affect your dreams.

For instance, I have noticed that most of the times we have nightmares because our concerns, issues, worries, disturbing thoughts, etc. are causing our ab to become heavy, which is impressed upon our *sahu*, and signals to our *ba* that our concerns and worries are a physical reality. While, we're on the subject. This is also the reason why it is important that you don't retire angry or with troubling thoughts on your mind. It is the same reason why if an individual says repetitively that they are stupid, dumb, a clodhopper, idiot, etc. or tells them self that they "can't" do something a number of times. The *ba* begins to take these limited beliefs and shape a limited reality. I'll never forget a situation that occurred to me, which I told in the MAA AANKH: Volume one that taught me about this truth. Real quick, I got a new car but didn't have insurance and was worried about getting into an accident. On my way to get auto insurance a young driver rear-ended me. It was definitely Murphy's Law.

The flipside is that, if you want to solve a problem or are trying to figure out how to achieve a specific goal, you can retire while asking repetitively "How to fix or solve X?" By simply repeating this question over and over again, it is impressed upon the *sahu* and signaled to the *ba*, which in return send the solution to the problem back to us in our dreams, an inspirational thought, an intuitive idea and even through someone else.

75

You can also repeat positive suggestions in the present tense like "I am healthy," "I am at peace," etc. until you fall asleep to create positive characteristics you want in your life.

A slight spin on this would be to draw a picture of what it is that you want before you retire. When you have finished drawing the picture, take the picture and burn the image inside of a cup. While the image is burning simply say, "Amen," which makes a very strong impression upon the *sahu* and allows your *ba* to focus on making your wish a physical reality.

As you can see, we can accomplish anything we want. Our ability to accomplish our dreams is only limited by our beliefs stored in our *sahu*.

Interpreting Night Dreams

Interpreting night dreams is a very simple process as well. Although there are thousands of dream interpretation books on the market, the best interpreter of your dream is you. Remember it is your *ba* that moves to KAMTA based upon what your *ab* is focused upon, so what you see may mean something completely different from what another sees because of the memories stored in your *sahu*.

Dreams are mystical, strange and weird because a lot of times we try to interpret them using reasoning. Again, it must be kept in mind that KAMTA does not have a structure, so our night dreams are going to be abstract, which is why we may find ourselves flying, talking to animals and doing all sorts of impossible feats in our dreams. I have found that the easiest way to interpret your night dream is to focus upon the meaning or how you would use the symbol that appears your night dream. If you would use a hammer to nail things together, to see a hammer in your dream would signify that you are trying to force things together. If you are walking up a flight of stairs in your night dream, it most likely signifies that you are trying to move up or advance in a particular situation. This is because night dreams reflect what we believe, feel and think. When you have interpreted the dream correctly, you will experience an inner knowing. This is when you can change your night dream.

By the way, if your night dream was not interpreted correctly, the *ba* will continue to hold on to the dream and it will usually stay on your mind until the meaning becomes clear. When this happens it is usually because we are stressed and too extroverted. I have found that it is best not to force the interpretation, but simply relax. When I have done this the meaning comes to me instantly or through some other medium. Like for instance, I will be having a conversation with someone and the meaning just pops into my awareness.

Changing Night Dreams

Since night dreams are a reflection of what we see, feel, believe and think, by implementing a change in how the dream plays out. We can influence various aspects of our life and also change our memories. There are several ways this can be done but I have found the most effective way to change a dream is by allowing the dream to continue and creating a new outcome. Let me give an example.

One night, I had a dream I was at a school and in the dream there was a young man whom I met that was showing me around. Now I knew the layout of the school but this young man was taking me around corners and behind back doors that I had never seen before. Then he led me to a stairwell that just kept descending downward. As I followed this young man down these stairs I noticed that the color of the walls and the floor had turned to a rich deep blue color. And it seemed like the farther we descended down the stairs, the darker blue the surroundings changed. But the stairwell changed and became like the insides of blue tiled cave that we were descending into. As we continued to climb down, I saw on the other side edges and stairs that were leading upward. Some of the people I saw on the other stairs were people whom I had cared about a long time ago and people I had known when I was younger. Finally, when we reached the bottom, there was a small fountain with water spilling out onto the floor. I remember as I stepped in the puddle, the young men told me, "Watch your step. It is slick." Then we started back on the other side. Where I was led to a tunnel and finally I awoke from the dream.

I wrote the dream down and immediately I understood that the young man in the dream was my Npu (whom you will meet in the next chapter) and the descending stairwell that I was being led down or into was KAMTA. The people on the other side of the stairwell or cave were people I cared about and individuals that I had met whom I hurt or had hurt me in my youth. The puddle of water that I stepped in was the mystical water of nyun. Because many of the people I saw in the dream I hadn't seen them for almost ten years or more and there was still some resentment that I had within. I knew the dream was a message from God telling me to let go of the past.

I changed the outcome of the night dream by imagining that I walked outside and met all the people that I saw in the dream. I then apologized to all these people that I had seen in the dream whom I had hurt and forgave those who harmed me. It was interesting because in the dream that I had created. I actually had dialogues with these individuals where they explained why they acted a certain way or I told them why I behaved in a particular manner. It was a true healing practice and because our ka is connected. I am quite certain that they received my apologies and I received theirs spiritually. When I had awakened from this created dream, I felt relieved and my heart was lighter.

All dreams and memories can be altered this same way. By learning how to change night dreams you learn how to develop self-confidence and self-esteem. I have found it to be a very effective tool for protecting yourself from intrusions as well, which I will explain in the next section on daydreaming.

Day Dreaming

I use to enjoy daydreaming as a kid because this was how I got my ideas on how to draw things. I didn't know it at the time but whenever I daydreamed I felt myself transported to another world. Then one day I remembered seeing one of those public announcements on television that if a child day dreamed too much it is possibly because they have a psychological problem. So in my young mind, refusing to be called retarded. I stopped daydreaming and when I caught myself daydreaming. I would break the trance by calling my attention back to focus. Fortunately, my ability to daydream was so strong that I could not deter it completely, so when I started experiencing hardships in my young adulthood. Certain types of music would lead me to enter into this trance state where I would be given a solution to the problem that ailed me at the time. It was only after accepting my calling that I began to learn the importance of daydreaming.

In the West there are a lot of misconceptions about daydreaming because most do not understand that dreaming is a form of communication with the Divine. It was not meant for us to solve all of the problems that exist in the world through earthly logic or reasoning alone. This is why this daydreaming ability was hardwired into our being, so that we could relax and escape the hardships of the physical world. By daydreaming we are able to actively move your *ba* into KAMTA to obtain a solution to whatever ails us. Daydreaming therefore is a very effect protective mechanism that we all have. In the previous section I indicated that by learning how to change your dreams you can protect yourself from all sorts of intrusions. This is because most people are not aware that thoughts and ideas are things. And most of the people who have heard this saying, don't truly understand how thoughts and ideas are things. As a result many people hold on to negative thoughts and ideas, which influence their actions and behaviors. Now most people in their right mind do not go around saying that they want to raise hell on earth and be the meanest son-of-a-gun they can be. They do however walk around with various anxieties, concerns, fears, worries, etc., which manifests itself in people actions, behaviors and criticism. Coincidentally, most people aren't aware when they are being critical, cynical or pessimistic because it has become a habit.

Ever wonder why when a suggestion is made to do something different. Generally speaking there are ten criticisms that appear to tear that suggestion down. It is because those individuals from a shamanic perspective are sharing a part in the same dream, which has caused them to share in the same physical reality. This dream that these individuals all share in is a type of thought-form, which we will discuss in the future.

I remembered when I started trying to get in shape and got back into running. I had some concerns about my knees. Like clockwork, it would seem there were several people I encountered that started talking about how they either needed knee surgery or had knee surgery. So, I had to change the subject quick fast and in a hurry! I didn't want to hear about that crap when I was trying to accomplish a goal. I was not going to be spooked and in one situation. I told the individual exactly that, "Stop trying to spook me!"

I was able to progress and I am still running today, but it because I had to take responsibility of my *ba*. The sad thing is, imagine how many people allow themselves to be spooked by their family, friends, the news media, infomercials, magazines, religion, movies, etc.

So daydreaming allows us to keep focused on our objective. It helps us mind what matters the most to us. When people don't tend to their own business, they are always in other people's business, worrying about anything and everything. Instead of being active human beings they become reactive and behave like animals, because their reasoning has gone out the door. This is why there are so many doomsday cults that exist and people stock piling for when 2012 or when God is going to come back. These people are all caught up in the same dream or nightmare. Thankfully this dream can be changed by simply creating a new outcome to your dream.

When you meet people who act and behave in a foul mood towards you or others, by focusing on them, you can tune into their ka and see the dream that is motivating their actions and behaviors. The image that comes to mind when you look at this individual will be the motivating force held by their ka. Sometimes by issuing a kind word or compliment can cause this individual's ka to grab hold to another dream, thereby, changing the individual's action and behaviors. Other times, a blessing or prayer sent to the individual through their ka may

80

be needed. To do this all that is required is that you imagine praying or giving the individual a blessing like some flowers, money, etc. or ask that God bless them. You will know if this practice is effective when you see the individual's physical response. Most of the time, this practice will produce immediate results, but if the individual's *ka* has been holding on to a certain dream for a long time (such as traumatic issues). It may require that the blessing be given to them numerous times.

Anything that you focus your attention upon will reveal the dream that it is inspiring or motivating it. All you have to do is simply focus upon the person or thing and it will reveal itself to you. By focusing upon an individual and seeing their dream doesn't mean you are reading their thoughts per se. You are simply able to see the dream or what's on their mind.

The same process can also be used to communicate with our body parts, because all of our body parts work together for the whole. Recall that memories are stored on several levels in our body as vibrations. Genetic memories for instance, are stored in our body on a cellular level, while learned memory is stored on a muscular level. The right motivation can trigger our body parts to relax and thereby release the associated memory. This can be achieved through daydreaming. All that is required is that you focus your attention on the body part. Then simply allow whatever you have to come to mind. All the sounds, images, smells, etc. that come to mind are ways in which your body parts are communicating to you or releasing the memory. When you communicate to your body parts, they can tell you when there is an imbalance or stress. Our body parts communicate to us all of the time whenever we have an adverse reaction to something we consumed. By actively communicating to them through daydreaming we can discover how to avoid certain foods and practices that may or may not contribute to our wellbeing. For instance, certain stimulation may occur from our heart telling us that we need to stop consuming or we need to consume more of a particular food, and so on.

Dreaming with Plants and Animals

You can also daydream with plants and animals. You just need to learn how to trust your intuition. It is said that inventor, botanist and famed scientist George Washington Carver did not have any books in his laboratory. Yet, he discovered over 300 uses for the peanut and 100 for the sweet potato. The only way he could have accomplished this is by communicating with these plants. Again, to those outside it would seem impossible but most of the early inventions were discovered this way. This is how herbs were found. The key however to communicating with plants and animals is that you have to respect them as living beings.

You must never forget that everything that physically exists has a *ba* and *sahu*. The only difference between human beings and all other beings is that we have a self-soul, which gives us the ability to exercise our will, but this doesn't mean that we are superior and all other beings are inferior or vice versa. History is full of examples of those that made such an assumption that has proven to be a costly one.

Plants and animals should be considered to be an extension of your spiritual family. They help us to achieve a particular goal and we help them as well. Life has always been about exchange and partnership with nature. For this reason, many first earth people understanding the relationship between plant, animals and humankind, personify plants and animals by calling them "Little Brother" or "Little Sister." It is not necessary for you to do this but when you personify plants and animals. You are less likely to abuse and misuse them. When you respect plants and animals, they will communicate to you as well through your daydreams.

Now, one of the simplest ways to begin communicating with plants is by learning how to care for an indoor plant. If you don't have a green thumb, it is perfectly okay, because this is a great way to develop one. Since, all plants to some degree require light, soil and water but the amount differs per plant. Learning how to care for a plant(s) is an excellent way to develop patience, reduce stress, and further develop your intuition, as you communicate with your plants. If you approach the matter from a fun but contemplative mindset, you will find that your plant after some time will tell you when it needs water, sunlight, etc. or has too much. Of course, it will not verbally tell you this, but you will get a hunch to water your plant or put it out in the sun, etc. You may also want to create a watering ritual by choosing a day to water your plants.

If communication between you and your plant is successful, your plant naturally will grow signifying that it is pleased with your efforts. If not obviously you still have to work on it. If your relationship with your plant is very successful you may get the hunch to purchase another plant or you might receive another plant as a gift from someone. From a higher perspective, this is your plant's way of signaling that you need to surround yourself with certain energies that you presently do not have to achieve your goals in life. This is how flowers and plants increase one's luck. It is not necessary that you borrow or imitate from another's culture when you rely upon your intuition. If you learn to trust your intuition your plant will communicate to you how it is meant to help you. A cactus plant for instance as well as pinecones will reveal that its purpose is to provide you with protective energy. While the scent of a, lavender plant will promote peace and relaxation.

Again respect your plant. Treat your plant, as you imagine it would like to be treated. Place it in a decorative pot that is encouraging and inspiring to you. If your plant outgrows the pot then find another container to hold it in.

Before we end this section, let's make one thing clear. Nothing can be substituted for good hard work. Just because you add a plant to your dwelling, take an herbal bath, etc. doesn't mean it is going to magically enhance your life and make all of your dreams come true. Sorry, it doesn't work like that. When I say that your luck will improve, I meant that you will receive greater inspiration that you have never had before. All you have to do is simply follow your intuition. For instance, you receive a cactus plant. It will radiate ideas of protection, which makes it an ideal plant to keep near your front door of your dwelling. Please don't leave your doors unlock because the cactus plant will protect you. Remember, earthly reasoning supports divine logic.

Study Questions

1. Which division of our spirit determines what is real and not real?
   The ba provides us with the divine knowledge and our sahu provides us with the earthly experience needed to physically succeed. But it is our ab that gives us the freedom to choose and therefore determines who and what we will be, along with what is real and not real.

2. According to the maa aankh, when does a new day begin and why?
   According to the maa aankh a new day begins at sunset the Ra Atum or "The Completed Ra" moment, because this is when we can begin to create a new life experience through our dreams.

3. Why is sunrise associated with the Khepera moment?
   Sunrise was referred to as Khepera "The Ra Coming Into Being" because it is the moment that physical things from out of the mysterious night come into existence.

4. The *Pert em Hru (Egyptian Book of the Dead)* and the Tibetan *Bardol Thodol* (the so-called Tibetan *Book of the Dead*) are mythical writings describing what and why?
   They are mythical writings that describe how to venture into the depths of KAMTA because KAMTA is a dark, mysterious and deep realm. If you do not have a clear purpose of venturing into KAMTA, you will easily lose your focus.

5. How do you recall your night dreams?
   The simplest method is to just write down what you remember word for word.

6. Why do we have nightmares?

We have nightmares because our concerns, issues, worries and disturbing thoughts are causing our *ab* to become heavy, which is impressed upon our *sahu* and signaled to our *ba* that our concerns and worries are a physical reality.

7. Why is it important that you do not retire after an argument, angry or with troubling thoughts on your mind?
   It is important you do not retire after an argument, angry or with troubling thoughts on your mind because this is impressed upon our *sahu* and hinted to our *ba* that this is the physical reality we want manifested in our life.

8. When we criticize ourselves (or others) repetitively by telling ourselves that we are stupid, dumb, a clodhopper, idiot, etc., or that "can't" do something, how do the divisions of our spirit respond?
   A negative impression is made upon the *sahu* which signals to the *ba* that our limited beliefs and experience is true, which convinces our *ab* that it is truth as well.

9. How do you solve problems through dreaming?
   You solve your problems through dreaming by simply asking repetitively "How to fix or solve X?" which will make a strong impression upon our sahu and signal to our ba to find a solution through divine means.

10. What are the limitations and restrictions from accomplishing our dreams and goals?
    The only limitations and restrictions we have preventing us from accomplishing our dreams and goals, are the limiting beliefs that we have in our *sahu*.

Exercise: How to Intentionally Dream

One of the easiest ways to make our dream a physical reality is through intentionally dreaming. When we intentionally dream we focus all of our attention on our objective, which causes the creative forces of our *ba* to make our dream a physical reality in TASETT. Now, understand that when I say that the creative forces will make our dream a physical reality. I do not mean that magically what we want it will appear before eyes. Hardly, what does happen is that a way will be made. If you wanted for instance a job, by focusing your intention on obtaining employment. You will in the course of looking for a job through the grapevine, will be led to get the type of job you always wanted. If you want a man or a woman, by focusing on having a loving and peaceful relationship, you will meet the right person for you. The reason this works is because instead of you relying upon your *sahu* you instead go to you *ba*, which knows what's best, because it is linked to the Divine. The more you focus upon your request, the more you ba presents it to Divine, until eventually the dreams becomes a physical reality.

It works by first and always deciding what it is that you want. Is it a better job? Is it better health? Are you tired of being alone and ready for a relationship? Whatever it is, create a clear, concise and distinct mental image of what you want and write it down on a piece of paper. From now on, imagine how you will feel when your dream has been achieved.

Next speak in the most optimistic way you can about your dream. When you go to bed at night imagine your dream accomplished. When you awake in the morning, imagine your dream accomplished. Adopt an attitude of gratitude by focusing on what you want and thinking of your dream as more like "when it happens" instead of "if it happens." Speak of your dream in the present tense because there is no time constraint in KAMTA. What you focus on today will become your future tomorrow. So, continue to imagine your dream becoming a physical reality.

86

Finally, if you don't put your dream into action, you are just a dreamer, so begin to make your dream a physical reality by acting towards your goal. You must put your dream into action so that when it manifests you are ready to receive it. You have to look forward to it coming and expect for your dream to be born like a newborn. When good parents receive news that they will be expecting a child, they don't start preparing for the child once it is born. They start as soon as they hear the news, so in the same sense. You have to do the same thing. Begin by drawing up a blueprint or a plan of how to make your dream a reality. Then hand it over so that your *ba* can provide insight on how you can make your dream a physical reality. Continue to act towards your goal by doing what today to create the future you want. Don't wait until the conditions are right to start living your dream. Act right now in the present so that your present actions will influence your future. Use the time you have right now to lead you to right place, the right people and right situation in order to have favorable conditions to make your dream a physical reality.

If you follow this formula you will find that there is no need to have fear. A lot of times we are afraid to ask for a raise on our job, a promotion, speak up for our self and take advantage of an opportunity and it is because we are not acting in accordance to the cycle of birth-life-death-rebirth. In other words, we are not in alignment with the Will of God. Understand it is not that God does not want us to have the things we want. It is that we are not doing things according to *maa*, in order to maintain and sustain the blessings given to us. Ever wonder why some people can have a blessing and lose it. It is a sad sight because they are clearly over their head. This is why we are all familiar with lottery winners who win millions of dollars and lose all of their money in a relatively short time. It is because they put out into KAMTA what they wanted (usually as a hope and wish) but didn't take the necessary steps to prepare for when the money arrived. If they had, they would have managed their money a lot better.

So, take the steps necessary to make your dream a physical reality by following the divine process. When you do you will appreciate and realize that like anything that is worth achieving. It is process and it doesn't always occur when we want it. Just like plants don't grow overnight, we have to nurture our dream into a physical reality through patience.

Whenever you begin to doubt or lack faith, remind yourself of your dream by imagining it already achieved. Next, express your gratitude for all the things that you are grateful for, for having the ability to create your future and for when your dream manifests. This will produce emotions of happiness that will drive away your fears and worry. Since our *sahu* stores memories associated with our feeling in our muscles, while doing this take your hands and raise them above your head. While imagining your goal make a clench fist (symbolizing holding on to your goal and bringing it out of KAMTA into TASETT) and say *amun*, which is Kamitic for conclusion, close, end or so be it[14].

During this time ignore all thoughts of negativity. Don't be fooled into believing that by ignoring negative images displayed in the media, negative beliefs portrayed by those around us, etc. means that you do not care and are being heartless. No one who was ill has ever got better by focusing on being ill. Just like I have never heard of the rich getting better by focusing on be in poverty. Life situations are changed when we focus on what we want and this is what you have to do to get what you want. So, if you are around people that are speaking negatively either change the subject or excuse yourself from the conversation. Remember, our *sahu* is very impressionable and the last thing we want is to doubt our dream becoming a physical reality.

Another thing I want to remind you is not to think or worry about how or when your dream with manifest. When you do this, you bring the dream into your awareness and take it out of KAMTA. Allow your *ba* to provide its king or queen with the knowhow and trust that it will do so.

---

[14] The word amun was borrowed from the Kamitic people by the founders of Judaism, Christianity and Islam. It was changed to Amen and this is the reason why it follows the end of most prayers.

CHAPTER 6

Creating Change Through the Power of the Will

You will free yourself when you learn to be neutral and follow the instructions of your heart without letting things perturb you.

Kamitic Proverb

It has been stated throughout this book that what makes us unique from all of the other beings that exist, is that we have been given an *ab*. It is because of our *ab* we have the ability to exercise free will. Through our will we are able to make choices and decisions that alter the way we live our life versus following our innate instincts. We can at will create a new way of achieving a goal, develop new processes or break any destructive habit that we desire. The reason most of us are plagued by our problems and aren't happy with our lives is because we don't understand how to use our will.

Most people don't understand that just telling yourself that you are going to exercise, stick to a diet or break a negative habit like smoking cigarettes, etc. doesn't work because, your will does not control that part of your being. The part of our being that controls everything from our autonomous nervous system to our physical body is our *sahu*. Our *sahu* does not know right from wrong, good from evil, left from right, etc. It only associates with what we feel. So, saying you want to exercise for all the right health reasons, break a negative habit or create a positive habit, is not going to work because talking to *sahu* is like talking outside of your being.

Another thing we need to understand in accomplishing any goal is that we cannot apply our will to something outside of our being. We can only apply our will within. Whenever you try to apply your will to something outside of your being, you are doing something that is unnatural and not supported by the Divine. This is the reason it does not work and in the rare cases when it does the results is usually disastrous. When we apply our will outside of our being, it is like forcing someone or something to be our slave.

To accomplish any goal you have to move focus upon your goal while moving your *ab* to the Amun Ra moment, so that what you want can be impressed onto your *sahu*. When you move your *ab* to the Amun Ra moment and stop trying to think and figure things out. Your *ba* will show you how to achieve your goal. You simply need to keep your goal on your *ab* so that it keeps reminding your *sahu* what it is that you want.

There is no need to project your will out on to some person or something. Your *ba* knows how to get anything and everything you want, because it is connected to KAMTA, which unites it to everything. When you try to project your will upon another it is like trying to make a relationship "happen." You can try as hard as you can but it will never work out and be prosperous. To accomplish any goal, all you need to do is give it direction by focusing intently upon what you want in order to motivate your *sahu* to assist you in achieving your goal. Understand there are no such things as a good or bad motivator, so long as it inspires you to achieve your goal.

Enemies of the Will

By relying upon our *ba* we can accomplish any dream that we have but doing so sometimes causes a lot of opposition to rise. This is because our *ab*, the very thing that makes us unique amongst all of the beings in existence, is very vulnerable especially when undeveloped. Remember we have to develop and strengthen our *ab*. We aren't born automatically knowing right from wrong; hot from cold, left from right, etc. we have to learn this, which means most of our life has controlled by our *sahu*. This is why it is so hard to break negative habits because we are in the "habit" of following the old pattern or paradigm that exists in our *sahu*. When you demand for something new, you are creating a new habit or paradigm for your *sahu*, which does not like change. So the enemy of our *ab* is any thought that tries to change our conscious course of action.

I never thought about this until one day someone asked me how I got good grades in my math classes when I was younger. It was funny a story because I remembered that I didn't always get good grades in math. I enjoyed mathematics and science both because when I was a kid my mother, who was an educator, used to make my brothers and I practice reading and doing math during our summer break. Even though we didn't have summer school, she was convinced that if children didn't practice their math and reading during the summer. Come autumn children would forget just about everything they learned in the previous months. It was a belief that she had acquired from my grandmother who had wanted to be a teacher. And even though she didn't finish school until much later, she made my mother practice her school work when she was younger. So, my brothers and I were next in line. As a result, we didn't have summer school but we had Mother School.

When I was in grade school I had relatively good grades in my math and science classes, but in high school. My math scores were not up to par and I couldn't figure out why. I ended up graduating in my favorite math class with a C average and I couldn't figure out what was my problem. When I got in college, I started having the same problem until it finally dawned on me that I was forgetting what I had previously learned. My mother was right and when I got in high school I stopped practicing my math, which was the reason I didn't do as well as I had wanted.

Deciding to turn the tables, I started practicing my math like I had done in elementary. I would work the same problems over and over until I could to the problems by memory. The interesting thing I noticed was that many of the college students I had met that had good math scores did the exact same thing. They also studied with other students that were focused on get good grades. It wasn't long after, that I began to study with these students as well. In the end, my test scores and grades dramatically improved. Since that time I go no less than 85% in any math class.

I forgot that I did any of this, so when I was retelling my story to a younger student. It was coming to me that the reason why I was successful was because I kept in my mind what I wanted, which was better math scores. I acted on what I wanted, which was to have better math scores. I ignored everything else and focused solely upon improving my scores, which led me to hanging out with people with like minds that were focused upon similar goals. Every student that I have found that has applied this same method has succeeded in his or her classes.

The enemies of our *ab* are those old thoughts and ideas that try to get us to follow the same old habits that were leading us nowhere. They are also the thoughts of others that could possibly derail what we want. This is why it is not enough to just hold on firmly to what we want. We have to act on it as well, which is a show of faith.

I saw the effectiveness of it by observing some people whom I knew that were diagnosed with cancer, like my mother and my wife's supervisor, overcome the illness and continue to live productive lives. I noticed that these individuals first made up in their mind that they wanted to live and were not going to be beat by the illness. Some of these individuals like my mother personified the illness by calling it the devil. They focused solely upon being healthy and ignored anything and everything that did not contribute to their wellbeing. They became totally optimistic individuals by focusing on seeing the positive aspects of life. When people entered into their presence with a negative disposition about life, they either were influenced by the positive energy radiating from these cancer survivors to the point that it changed their outlook or they were forced to leave. Out of the cancer survivors that I noticed that used this method. They are continuing to live and are still cancer free. They simply made their body uninhabitable by these organisms.

I have since this time applied this method to other areas of my life. As I mentioned in *MAA AANKH Volume 1*, I believe part of the reason I became ill was because I was focused upon not becoming ill. I adopted a dietary lifestyle, partook in health practices, etc. all for the wrong reasons. I listened and followed so-called health gurus' talk about what my body needed and how this food and that food was not good for me. It was following what others were telling me, whose health information was constantly contradicting and conflicting with other so-called health gurus. In the end, it came down to a matter of opinion and advertising dollars. I don't think that my diet was the sole culprit of body's breakdown but I seriously believe the stress caused by it did not help. Years later, I now admit that the whole approach was totally un-holistic, because none of it included the input of my *ba*. I should have simply focused upon being healthy and maintaining my ideal weight. This way I could allow my *ba* to connect me and lead me in the right direction to being healthy.

I noticed after observing others and applying this method that in order to be victorious using it. Sometime, you have to disassociate yourself with people and things that are not supportive of your goal. Now, let me make this clear because there is a misconception circulating around that by ignoring the news, tabloids and other forms of media (and individuals) that appear negative. That one is being heartless, cruel and superficial because they are ignoring reality. No. The purpose of ignoring all of this is to purge your self of the negative imagery so that you can concentrate and contribute to society.

You can't become healthy and help others become healthier is you are focusing upon illness. The only way to be healthy is to focus upon being healthy and allowing your *ba* to guide you to that goal by associating with healthy people. This is the only way you can help people who are in an unhealthy state.

The same can be said about money. From all of the wealth books I have read and some of the wealthy people I have met. They have never revealed that they made their money focusing on poverty. The only way rich people became rich is by doing what other rich people have done, which is learning the language of business. This is the only way to help those in poverty as the saying goes, "Give a man a fish he'll eat for a day. Teach him how to fish and he'll eat forever."

So, you have to ignore the naysayers and that may mean turning off the television, ignoring the news, closing your eyes to the tabloids at the supermarket until your *ab* is strong enough to get what you want.

Study Questions

1. Why can't you break a negative habit like overeating, cigarette smoking, gossiping, etc. or create a positive habit like exercising, studying, etc., by telling yourself to do so?
   You cannot create or break a habit by telling yourself because we are creatures of habit, which means what we want has to be repetitiously impressed upon our *sahu*.

2. How do you impress what it is that we want upon our *sahu*?
   The only way to impress what we want upon our *sahu* is by focusing on something that invokes our emotions.

3. Would wanting to look good in your clothes and feel good about your body be a good goal to focus upon for an individual desiring to lose weight? If so, why?
   Yes. Wanting to look good in your clothes and feel good about your body, would be a good goal to focus upon for an individual desiring to lose weight. The reason is because any goal can be used as a motivating factor to help propel you to achieving your goal. There is no right or wrong motivator, so long as it inspires you.

4. When it comes to achieving our goals. What is the sole purpose of the *ab*?
   The sole purpose of the *ab* when it comes to achieving our goals is to keep whatever we want on our *ab*.

5. Does the *sahu* reason?
   No. The *sahu* is logical but it does not reason. It does not know right from wrong. It associates everything that we know through our feelings of pain and pleasure.

6. Can you apply your will to someone in order to make him or her do what you want?
   No. You cannot will someone to do what you want. Trying to do so is not only wrong but also a waste of time and energy.

94

7. How do you get others to assist you in achieving your goals?
   You don't. All you need to is lay upon your *ab* what it is that
   you want and allow your *ba* to connect you to the right people.

8. What happens when you try to force your will upon another?
   It is like trying to make a relationship "happen." You can try as
   hard as you can but it will never work out and be prosperous.

9. Why is it important that you when you focus upon what you
   want that you move your *ab* to the Amun Ra moment?
   When you move your *ab* to the Amun Ra moment, you stop
   thinking and focusing upon how to achieve your goal. And,
   instead allow your *ba* to provide you with a solution on how to
   achieve your goal.

10. What are the enemies of the will and how do you protect
    yourself from them?
    The enemies of the will are any contrary and conflicting belief,
    idea and thought that can discourage and deter us from
    achieving our goal. The only way to protect our *ab* from them is
    by not giving them any time or energy by simply ignoring them
    (newspapers, tabloids, television, negative people, etc.)

Exercise: How to Strengthen the Power of Your Will

The old folks use to say, "An idle mind is the devil's workshop,"
because even though they may not have known the scientific term.
They understood that if you did not tend to the *sahu*. It would not
remain idle and it would instead use its limited experience and
understanding to find something to entertain itself, which most likely
would be something negative. Remember, our *sahu* functions
automatically, whether we choose to tend to it or not. So, to keep the
enemies of the will at bay all you have to do is create a clear and
concise image of what we want.

That's it. It is that simple, but what makes it hard is functioning
on a day-to-day basis because of the people we encounter.

This is the hard part, because most people think by saying they want to break a negative habit, overcome an illness, have greater success on their job, salvation, etc. that it is just going to happen. Unfortunately, it doesn't work this way. This is the reason why after preaching a fiery and long sermon on Sunday, most of the pious the following day lose their Holy Ghost. It is because you cannot change behavior by simply talking to your *sahu*. You have to "pray without ceasing," which means constantly and steadily holding the vision of what you want in your mind's eye everyday. You have to constantly imagine how it will feel to have achieved your goal. You have to keep this image in your mind at all time, so that there is no doubt that it will not manifest. This means if possible daydreaming about you want even in your spare time.

Along with keeping your vision of what you want on your *ab* or mind's eye. You also have to act towards making your vision a physical reality. If you want better grades then you need to act towards getting better grades, while focusing on your vision. If you want a better relationship, you need to act as if you have a good relationship, while focusing on what you want. The *ba* will provide you with the inspiration you need to accomplish your will. Don't worry how, remember this is a mystery, just know that it will and act towards it.

Finally, while you are doing this be sure to express your gratitude. When you express your gratitude for what you have, it naturally generates a feeling of happiness within, which is closely associated with the *maa*. By expressing your gratitude for what you have received or haven't received. You are creating a spiritual situation for a blessing to be given to you. Always, express your gratitude because it helps to keep you at peace.

It is very important that when you are minding your business that you guard your speech by tailoring your words towards your objective. This can be a challenge to do because we are creatures of habit and many people are in the habit of complaining about how they feel, but it is possible. Instead of speaking from a TASETT perspective, speak from a KAMTA perspective. By this I mean instead of seeing the glass as half empty change your perspective and see it as half-full. For

96

instance, don't talk about how bad you feel. Instead talk about how you are looking forward to relaxing, enjoying your life, etc.

If you are trying to recover from an illness the worst thing you can do is read literature about the illness, because your *sahu* will remember it and inform your *ba* that the information is truth and final. It will therefore contradict and conflict with your *ab*. Instead focus your thoughts on what is that you want. Understand that if you are in pain recognize that the pain is part of the healing process. If need be take the necessary fomentation, medication, etc. prescribed by a certified and licensed health professional to alleviate the pain, but continue to express your gratitude, faith and focus your will on your objective.

Please note if your body was inflicted with ill-ness for a long time. It may take longer to recover only because the ill-ness has become a familiar habit of the *sahu*, but don't be discouraged. All habits can be broken through with proper application of the *ba*.

When people come to you complaining about their woes, you do not need to be cold, heartless and unconcerned. You do need to understand that you have your life to live and they have their life to live. So, offer words of encouragement by changing the subject with uplifting conversation. If you are unable to do so, you need to politely excuse yourself because failure to do so might cause your will to stray.

Staring Death in the Face

Another way to strengthen your will, help you to decide what you want is to do, as well as discover what your true passions are in life, is to stare death in the face and write a mock obituary. For some, I am pretty sure this sounds a little macabre but the idea is that if you write down how you want people to remember you when you die. You are in a way creating the future that you want. So begin by writing down all of your accomplishments, achievements and list all of the things that you want to do. Include in your list, places you want to visit and how people would remember you. Write down the things you enjoyed and what you disliked the most and how you resolved them.

By laying this upon your *ab*, you resolve within yourself that you have already accomplished what you want. Since the *ba* only focuses on the present. This sets things up so that you are focused upon maintaining what you already have; instead of trying to obtain your goals. Through this exercise, you will also see your passions along with your destiny. If for instance, you would like to be remembered as being a mild manner and powerful leader. You will see that you enjoy hearing speakers and value the character traits good leaders have, which are qualities you have but need to maintain or fine tune.

It is always a good idea to read over your mock obituary once in a while. I try to read over mines every time it is my birthday, to see how close or far off I am. The thing to remember about this is that you should not obsess over it. Everything will happen in its due season. If you have a different understanding of life and want to change your mock obituary then do so. It is your life. You have the right to change any aspect of your life that you do not approve of.

This technique can be applied to any endeavor you set your mind on. You simply begin by clearly stating what it is that you want accomplished in the past tense. For instance, if you are a student and you want to receive an "A" out of your class. Then you would begin by resolving that you already have an "A" so you just need to find a way to keep it. If your objective was recovering from an illness, then you fix in your mind that you are already healed. You just need to go through the steps of maintaining your good health, which will already put you in proper frame of mindset of doing things as if you were healthy. You may want to get an old photo of yourself when you were happy and use it for motivation.

This is a very powerful technique when applied correctly. I use to do this before I met Iya, which helped me to escape some dangerous situations I found myself in when I was younger. It was later after I met Iya that she told me that numerous spiritual people and successful professional have used this method for the same purpose.

CHAPTER 7

Creating Change With Your Guardian Spirits

Men need images. Lacking them they invent idols. Better then to found the images on realities that lead the true seeker to the source.

Kamitic Proverb

It has been found that at least half of the world population believes in the existence of angels, guardian angels and other spiritual beings, but what are angels? Are they real? Do they really exist or are they a figment of our imagination? All of these questions and more will be answered in this chapter.

Angels since time immemorial have existed in every culture. Angels have been called everything from deities, gods, goddesses, daemons, to forms and archetypes by people all over the world. But they all act as messenger and guardian beings. Most non-Western cultures see these spiritual beings as entities that they need to develop a partnership with through veneration, but not in West. The reason a relationship is discouraged between human beings and angels in the West is because there is a gross misunderstanding about these spiritual beings due to a lack of knowledge of self. So we must recall that according to Genesis 1:26, which states:

> *And God said, Let us make man in our image, after*
> *our likeness: and let them have dominion over the*
> *fish of the sea, and over the fowl of the air, and over*
> *the cattle, and over the earth, and over every*
> *creeping thing that creepeth upon the earth.*

The biblical passage clearly states that man and woman are supposed to be gods and goddesses because we are the only beings were created in the image of God. For a lot of people this statement is very controversial but the biblical text is clear and other examples can be found throughout the Bible. Such as in Psalms 82:6-7, which states:

> *I have said, Ye are gods; and all of you are children*
> *of the most High. But ye shall die like men, and fall*
> *like one of the princes.*

Part of the reason man and woman's divinity is so debated is because many believe that we were created under the angels because of sloppy translation. For instance, in Psalms 8:4-5 which reads according to the *King James Version* of the Bible:

> *What is man, that thou art mindful of him? And the*
> *son of man, that thou visitest him?*
> *For thou have mast him a little lower than the*
> *angels, and has crowned him with glory and honor.*

But, according to *Strong's Exhaustive Concordance of the Bible*, everywhere you see the word God, in the Old Testament; it actually is *elohim* in the Hebrew language. In fact, the word *elohim* is used around 2,250 times throughout the Old Testament, and what's even more interesting about the word *elohim*. Is that it is used in place of the word "angels" and "gods" because *elohim* is plural for *eloah*, but the name of God in the Hebrew language is Yahweh. This means the actual translation of Psalms 8:4-5 should read as in the *New American Standard Bible*:

> *What is man, that Thou dost take thought of him?*
> *And the son of man, that Thou dost care for him?*
> *Yet Thou hast made him a little lower than God and*
> *dost crown him with glory and majesty!*

Man and woman weren't created lower than the angels. We were created under God and in God's image, which means the angels were created to serve us. This misunderstanding about man and woman's divinity and our connection to God caused the translators of the bible to sidestep in their translation because they didn't understand

100

what they were reading. They were basing their understanding of the spiritual truths in the bible upon their *sahu*. This is why Hebrew 1:14 in regards to spiritual entities is presented as a question that asks:

> *Are they not all ministering spirits, sent forth to*
> *minister for them who shall be heirs of salvation?*

When it should be more like a statement as presented in the New Living Translation, of Hebrews that affirms:

> *Therefore, angels are only servants--spirits sent to*
> *care for people who will inherit salvation.*

When it is understood that we are made in the image of God and that the angels were created to serve us, it becomes clear why the devil of Christian lore has been vying for the human soul and winning. It also explains the reason why the forces of evil fascinate so many people and so many religious people fear the devil; yet claim to have the power of God.

It is because if we don't know that we were created to be gods and goddesses like the Divine whose image we were made out of. Yet, the devil knows. We can easily be taken advantage of due to our ignorance and encouraged by any force to do a number of things under the guise that we are doing God's work. Can you now see the danger of not having knowledge of self? We will return back to this subject as to how the devil is able to manipulate us.

Understanding that we are made in the image of God and that the angels were created to serve us means, that the angels, gods, spirits, archetypes (or whatever you want to call them) are ambassadors, emissaries or messengers between God and us. It also implies that since we made in the image of God and are a microcosm of the Macrocosm. That just like the Universe is composed of positive and negative forces. We as human beings also have positive and negative forces that exist within and outside of our being.

If we keep in mind what was said about the divisions of our spirit and remember that when our *ab* is moved to the Amun Ra moment of time. We are no longer dependent upon our experiences stored in our *sahu*, because we now have access to KAMTA through our *ba*. It becomes apparent that these spiritual beings have always existed all around us. The reason we never noticed them is because most of us have been taught not to trust this part of our being. But, when we begin to depend upon *ba*, we will soon discover that these spiritual beings exist and can assist us in every aspect of life, like the famed author Napoleon Hill learned.

For those of you who do not know who Mr. Hill is, he is considered to be one of the founders of the personal-success writings of today. Hill was born to a poor family in the Appalachian mountain of Southwest Virginia. When he was a teenager he became a reporter for one of the small town newspapers and saved his earnings to attend college, but due to financial reasons had to withdrawal. Then a pivotal moment in his life occurred around 1908 when he met Andrew Carnegie, considered to be one of the wealthiest men in the world at the time, who gave Hill a very interesting assignment. It was to outline a formula for success by interviewing the most famous and wealthiest people of the time like automaker Henry Ford, Thomas Edison, Alexander Graham Bell and many others. After doing so, Hill was encouraged to implement the theories that he learned from these affluent individuals, into his life to assure that they worked. Hill applied what he learned from these interviews, which led to him writing his most popular book to this day, which has been reprinted several times over in several languages is called *Think and Grow Rich.*

Hill discovered a lot of interesting ways that helped him to achieve success. One of the most fascinating methods he discussed in his works was that he would fall asleep and have a meeting with famous men, whose attributes and qualities that he admired, and ask these men in his imagination to teach him how he could incorporate these same attributes in his daily living. Hill called these men he met within his imagination the *(Nine) Invisible Counselors.* Hill stated that after several months of doing this he noticed that these characters would become more and more real. He states that although these

102

characters originated as puppets of his imagination they had evolved to the point that they took on personalities of their own and engaging in dialogue with each other. These counselors had become so real that Hill said that he had to abstain from using them at times just to remind himself that they were a product of his imagination. When he continued to use them, Hill claims that these counselors guided him through emergencies and helped him with every difficult problem that he and his clients faced.

How Are Guardian Angels Created?

There are many theories as to how these spiritual beings were created. Some believe that they were created by God to assist in the creation of the Universe. Others believe that these spiritual beings came into existence after God self-created Him/Herself. I personally believe based upon my understanding that we are all spiritual beings infused into a physical body, that these entities are ancestral beings.

Before I explain my theory on the subject, it must be remembered that history teaches us that whenever two cultures encounter each other through conquest. The dominant culture usually extracts from the subjugated the more constructive aspects of its culture. As a result, the people who have been subdued will either willingly or by force adopt the dominant culture as their own, while ignoring their cultural significance, but the culture of the subdued will not go quietly. It will continue to survive (even as an afterthought) until its people has no further need of it. If ever the needs of the subjugated people becomes so great that the culture of the dominant people cannot and will not provide. The culture or the spirit of the subjugated people will rise.

I am recounting this from the beginning of the book because this is what happened to me when I was younger. And it is one of the reasons I found it difficult to fully embrace Western religion. It is due to the life after death concept, which is the cornerstone of many African (and non-Western) spiritual traditions. Because the African theology of the soul did not survive in North America, but the belief and experience did. An internal conflict persisted within me and fueled my desire to embrace my own cultural beliefs.

For instance, I remember growing up as a child and being taught that when we die. We will go to our earthly graves and then on Judgment Day if we were good. God will judge us and we will ascend to the heavens, but if we were evil we would go hell. This Western theology conflicted with my African derived "common knowledge" cultural upbringing that revealed to me that some children are born as "old souls," meaning they have previous knowledge and experience of life as newborns. Let me give you an example.

I have a niece who at the time of this writing is two years old. She chews her food, acts and has mannerisms like an old woman. She is a very intelligent child that loves music, but has a lot of personality and is very ornery. By Western belief there is no way that she could have learned in her two years of living on the planet, all of these characteristics that fast. Where did she get these characteristics? Western theology (excluding Spiritualism) could not explain this phenomenon to me when I was younger and cannot provide an answer now, because Western beliefs are linear and are based upon observable and limited physical experiences.

Only African and other non-Western theology were able to present to me possible theories as to why this phenomenon exists, because they don't attempt to justify such occurrences as Westerners do. They simply accept that is and incorporate it into their beliefs through myth in order to expand upon their understanding of life. It is interesting that African and other non-Western belief systems concur with the kabalistic belief that the legendary Enoch was transformed into an angelic being Metatron, according to their philosophy. While most Westerners on the other hand debate this concept because they need physical and literal proof in order to accept it. African and non-Western belief systems don't require physical proof all the time just to accept a belief. It just simply needs to make sense in order for it to be practical in order to further and support their spiritual understanding. This is what makes African and non-Western belief systems circular or holistic because it consists of observable physical experiences, as well as well as experience with spiritual phenomenon.

Consciousness and Reincarnation

To explain why so many children are born as "old souls" based upon my experience and research into the esoteric teachings of Kamit. It is because remember we are physical creatures infused with the *Spirit*. The main divisions of our Spirit are the *ba, sahu* and *ab*, which is more like a reference to consciousness. I will not repeat everything that was said earlier about these divisions. I will only state what happens to these divisions of the spirit when an individual dies.

Keeping in mind that our *ba* (divine conscious) was created and given to us by God and is directly connected to our breathing. And since every living thing on the planet shares in the same breath, the *ba* connects us to every living being that exists and thereby connects us to God. The purpose of the ba is to provide every living being a purpose for existing, so to accomplish its objective. The *ba* draws from the spiritual nature of the Universe or the KAMTA all of the spiritual attributes needed for a living being to spiritually survive and have a new experience. The *ba* basically grants every living being with a new personality, so that every being can enjoy and learn from its present experience. The *ba* accomplishes its goal by residing on top of our head and providing all living beings, a khu (divine wisdom), *shekhem* (divine power) and *ren* (our divine name/destiny) at birth, which provides for us everything from our physical appearance, health, social and economic status including the various challenges we will be faced that relate to our destiny. If we were not given a new *ba* at birth, we would never rest for one and would already know how events would play out in life. This would be like repeating the same level in grade school forever, with no rest in sight and never evolving from the experience. It is because the *ba* exists solely to provide us with the purpose for living, when it expires. The physical body dies because it has no reason to exist, so when one physically dies. The *ba* returns back to the spiritual nature of the Universe.

The *sahu* (physical-body conscious) was created and given to us by God. The purpose of the *sahu* you may recall is to help us to physically survive. It fulfills this objective like the ba by drawing from another, but instead of the drawing upon the spiritual nature of the Universe. The sahu draws upon the physical nature of the Universe or the TASETT, all of the physical attributes needed for a specific living being to physically survive. The sahu basically grants every living being with a new body in order to withstand tragedy, loss, injury, illness, misfortune, etc. To accomplish its goal, the *sahu*, which governs all of our genetic memories and resides near the base of every living being, provides all living beings with a khab (physical body), khabit (emotions and instincts) and a ka (personality) at birth. Everything that physically exists has a *sahu*, so when the *ba* expires the *sahu* has fulfilled its purpose and ceases to exist. Like the ba, the *sahu* returns back from where it came from in the physical Universe. There in nature the *sahu* waits to be reincarnated by following the genetic memories it has stored in the previous life. It is from these memories the *sahu* is able to recreate a new physical body with all of the physical resemblance from the past. This is how various species of animals are created. It is the *sahu* that gives us our hair, eyes, etc. to our mannerisms that resemble a distant relative, but our *ba* that makes us distinct beings. In animals it is the *sahu* that gives specific species a certain characteristic, color; pattern, etc., while the *ba* makes them unique creatures.

What makes human beings unique amongst all of the living beings is that we have an *ab*, which was given to us by God, so that we can choose the type of life we want to live. The *ab* (human consciousness) gives us the ability to learn through observation and make decisions based upon the unlimited opportunities provided by our *ba* and the limited experiences provided by our *sahu*. The ab allows us to see beyond the physical, which is the reason why all human beings perceive something after death regardless if we can explain it or not. It is for this reason; unlike animals we bury our dead instead of leaving them exposed to elements and ravenous beasts of the planet.

Although all three divisions are essential for our survival, it is the *ab* that is the most important for our development because the choices we make and the consequences of our actions, determines the fate of our life and the future state of our existence. This is because the consequences of our actions are determined by the *maa*, which mirrors what exists above below. It is from this observation that we are able to learn from our present-day experiences and make the necessary changes. So, when the *ba* expires and returns back to the spiritual nature of the Universe and, the *sahu* after fulfilling its purpose returns back to the physical nature of the Universe. It is the *ab* that continues to exist and survive death because it is the eternal part of our being that we share with God, which has allowed us to learn based upon observation and reasoning.

So, immediately after death, the deceased lingers around his or her corpse for a short time until it is time for them to pass into the otherworld. The reason the deceased does this I am told is because the deceased is curious to know what the living thought about them in order to clear his or her conscience. Just like in life, in order for us to advance to this next grade, level, understanding, etc. we have to have mastered the level we are on. Our conscious has to have evolved or learned from the experience, so that whatever wrong was committed will not be repeated. The *maa* mirrors this exact experiences in death, so the deceased has to have a clear conscience in order to pass into the other world or KAMTA with a light ab. It is only then that the deceased can move to the next level of existence, which occurs with the *ab* of the deceased reincarnating into another life form. This entire process is allegorized as the Kamitic *Weighing of Words*.

What Happens After Death?

The deceased based upon the lightness of their ab will become one of three types of spirits called an *aapepu, aakhu* or *netcharu.*

The Aapepu: The Malevolent Spirits of the Dead

If the living remembers the deceased as being a horrible individual that authored massive scales of violence and chaos. These individuals that preyed upon their fellow human beings like wild animals, would be called beast man or woman because they acted and behaved as if they had no conscience. Although man and woman both have the ability to commit great acts of evil because it is a matter of choice. The extreme heaviness and enormous amount of guilt that would fall upon our *ab* prevents most people from doing so, except for the one known as Set.

Set the Ruler of Evil

Set who later became known as Set-an and Satan in Christian lore, was a murderer, thief, excellent propagandist, manipulator, tyrant, warmonger and witch. He was so successful in his chaotic and destructive quest for power that he was immortalized. He is forever known as the author of confusion, evil, storms, violence and war. He has his hands in every physical affair because he was the original ruler of TASETT and after the Great War (which will be discussed in the *Story of Osar*) he was forced to surrender and banished back to the desert. Set is the Great Deceiver and his greatest trick to date, is convincing people that real devil worshippers bow down before goat looking images. It is this fallacy that has allowed Set to persuade people into committing unspeakable heinous acts through fits of rage, greed, jealousy and selfishness.

Don't be fooled into believing that God and Set (the devil) are bitter enemies locked in an eternal battle of good versus evil. And, don't be hoodwinked into believing that Set is some impish being running around with a pitchfork stealing souls. Set is a spirit that exists within and outside of us all. We give him power whenever we rely solely upon our *sahu* to solve our problems. Remember, the experiences of our *sahu* are limited because they are based upon the limited physical aspects of the Universe. This is the source of Set's power.

There are people that have tried to devote their life to committing evil but usually Aummit, the great devourer is sent to fetch their ab. As a result, these individuals upon feeling the enormous pain brought on by their conscience said to be similar to a heart attack but much worst. Are coaxed into committing suicide, in order to escape the intense agony that they feel. This act seals their fate and the Great Devourer, which is part lion, hippopotamus, leopard and crocodile monster, known as the Beast in Christianity, who was the Kamitic equivalent to the boogey man. Devourers the *ab* of the wicked preventing the deceased like Hitler from ever returning back to the land of the living and inflicting havoc upon humankind. Fortunately, this is rare and is a worst-case scenario.

For most deceased, if the living remembers them as being a confused, hostile, envious individual or a troublemaker that engaged in social misconduct, such as theft, adultery, murder, drug dealing, witchcraft, etc. Then the deceased will have a heavy *ab*, (not as heavy as the previous unfortunate soul) which will prevent them from passing into KAMTA.

Understand, we all make mistakes and everyone has a past, but it is because of our *ba*. We all have the divine ability to improve our life and wellbeing by righting our wrongs, learning from our mistakes and rising to become a better individual. A lot of times, the motivating factor behind our better judgment are the consequences of our actions. We therefore know that we will all physically die some day, which most people don't fear. It is the manner in which we will physically die that frightens us the most.

Typically, the deceased with a heavy *ab* has died suddenly, violently, without a proper burial or prematurely by committing suicide, which is usually due to their confused, misguided and unwise decisions that they made in life. Many of these spirits for the most part allegorically speaking lived by the sword and died by the sword. It is because the choices these people made in life attracted chaos, confusion and destruction. Generally they were shunned from the family and the community, because they leeched upon their brothers and sisters. Since what we do in life is reflected in death, these individuals as ghosts and haunts continued to leech upon the living, which is why they are called aapepu (snakes or worms, hence parasites).

Unable to pass into KAMTA and continue their evolution, the aapepu remain earthbound. So they return to the places (homes, bars, clubs, alleyways, etc.) that they frequented in life and haunt them with their presence.

The aapepu are usually the culprits behind every accidents, obstacle, illnesses, misfortunes and psychological disturbances. Like a viper crossing along the path, they make you take notice of them because if you don't you will get bit with their poison. Most people if they are generally healthy, happy, have a good relationship with their family, enjoy their job and generally content with life. They are not affected and can generally ignore the misguided, negative and unwise influences of the aapepu, which is like ignoring a very annoying and loud salesperson. It is usually those whose *ab* is undeveloped like children or has become vulnerable through the misuse of substances (alcohol or drugs), depression or illness that become victims of the aapepu.

Usually you can detect when you have encountered an aapepu because you will all of a sudden feel a rush of anxiety, dread or sadness for no apparent reason. Other times you might feel like your hair is standing up on your neck, you may have an eerie cold sensation or an extremely hot sensation. This is all proof that the aapepu are stuck either in or around TASETT, being a desert TASETT (hell) gets both extremely hot and cold.

To Drive Away Aapepu

To drive an aapepu off of you and away from your dwelling, you have to remind yourself that this is your body and your life. Dream your body parts to resist the foreign influence and command them to take back control of your body. Then get some salt and jump into the bathtub. While standing in the bathtub vigorously rub salt on your head, neck, and shoulders, down your arms, in your hands, down your stomach, genitals, along your thighs, knees and finally to your feet, while demanding and screaming to the negative spirit to get off of you. When you have finished. Take buckets of cold water and throw it at the salt in the bathtub, while yelling at the aapepu to return back to the hole it climbed out peacefully. If you need to, while standing in the bathtub with your clothes on. Turn on the cold water while scrubbing with salt or if you have access, go jump in the ocean. All of these steps will send a serious shock to your system and help you dislodge the spiritual parasites' grasp.

Once you have finished. Make a repelling mixture with 1 part salt and 3 parts ground up camphor blocks or if you can't find any camphor use mothballs. Then sprinkle this mixture in all of the corners of your house in a counter clockwise direction according to the maa aankh starting from your front door. Then sweep the salt up in a clockwise direction, which is like erasing one's steps. Then discard the salt as far away from your home as possible. It is recommended that you throw it running water moving away from your home, but if this is not available. Then discard the salt by throwing it in the toilet or into the sewer with same demands. Then return back home using a different route. If your dwelling is carpeted then vacuum up the salt and discard it the same way explained above. Next, let some sunshine in your home. Open the windows, burn frankincense incense, buy some fresh flowers and place them all around your house. Simply follow your intuition. To protect your dwelling from aapepu will be discussed at the end of the chapter.

The Aakhu: Our Personal Spirit Guides

If the living remembers the deceased as being a benevolent individual, then the deceased can safely pass into the otherworld (and continue in their evolution) with a light ab or clear conscience. The deceased at this moment assumes a white body (the color of purity) and becomes an ancestral spirit called an aakhu.

I have tried to understand what is the true purpose of an ancestor according to ancient African theory because in contemporary times. People have used the word to describe any biological relative that has died and in many of the Afrospiritual traditions I have encountered. The term is applied to biological relatives, heroes, heroines, cultural icons, and even children. The other thing I found interesting about ancestors in the Afrospiritual traditions was that it all had something to do with ethical living, so I wanted to know what really is an ancestor, how does one become an ancestor, why are they

111

so important to many non-Western practices and what makes them uniquely different from aapepu. I remembered at the time I asked this question no one was able to answer it for me or I was not able to truly understand what I was being told. Then one day I received a flash of insight and was shown that it relates to the *ab* of the individual.

I was reminded we are all given an *ab* to make choices and decisions. Then I began to see that is was through the choices and decisions that we make that strengthens our *ab*, as well as reflects who we really are. It became apparent to me that a true ancestor can be any deceased man, woman, young or old that chose during their lifetime to do the right thing even in the face of danger. To be able to do the right thing even in the face of danger (even when people aren't looking) takes courage, discipline, inner strength and power, hence a light (clear conscience/ethical), powerful and very strong *ab*.

The man or woman that knows the science of the maa knows that if they live a courageous, self-discipline and righteous life. They will have a strong ab, which will cause a powerful positive shift in the dynamics of all affairs, especially in regards to their individual dealings. This is the reason why even heroes, heroines and martyrs who demonstrate a strong degree of selflessness, after dying from the hands of another are still able to become aakhu. It is because they are remembered for their bold, ethical, courageous and righteous living. Even some infants that have died prematurely can be said to have made self-sacrifices in order to teach the living about the value of life. The aakhu through their selflessness lived and made sacrifices for the benefit of their family, community, people, etc. Whereas the aapepu through generally had no real concern for others, so they preyed upon others (like beast do) for their own selfish benefit and gratification, which is why their actions and behaviors were so disruptive.

These are all examples that make the aakhu uniquely different from the aapepu who were generally selfish and were only concerned about their own wellbeing while living

It can be said, that God allows these spirits to be honored, remembered and venerated like Christian saints in death. In order to remind the living that even though life is very fragile, it is righteous living that echoes our deeds throughout the heavens and the earth. In other words, it is righteous living that guarantees eternal life because the soul of the deceased continues to live on in the minds of the living and therefore in the heavens.

Ancestor veneration, which includes but is not limited to remembering the dead on a specific day (holiday), commemorating them through the building of monuments, memorials, masquerades, parades, etc., therefore, is the oldest spiritual practice mainly because God finds no fault with it.

The clear and distinct difference between the aapepu and aakhu besides the fact that the former is considered to be a ghost, while the latter is considered an ancestor, is due to the choices that they made. The aapepu while in life made choices that caused them to be ostracized from their family, community and people. The aakhu on the other hand made choices that caused them to honored and venerated. Metaphorically speaking it can be said that both were snakes but the aakhu were able to shed their clothing and enter into a new state of existence, leaving behind a white shell. In other words, they were transformed through their righteous living into something white and pure. Righteous living is the true definition of the maa aankh.

It is for this reason, the aakhu are the first residents to dwell in KAMTA and they are the first spirits that we encounter because we knew many of them before they died. This makes our aakhu closer to us than any other spirit, and they are the first to be honored. It is in our times of uncertainty the aakhu visit us in memory because our aakhu are still concerned about their descendants. All aakhu are spirit guides that inspire and encourage righteous living. Since one can be encouraged to live righteously in a number of ways, there are many types of aakhu that exist. Some of the more commons ones honored and venerated are:

- **Biological Aakhu,** are our deceased relatives that encourage the maa aankh within our family. This group includes the souls of infants and children that have died before the age of reasoning.

113

- **Historical Aakhu,** are deceased heroes and heroines that encourage the maa aankh along historical lines. These are aakhu that have made history and have named in their honor buildings, streets, monuments, etc.

- **Cultural Aakhu,** are similar in many ways to historical aakhu but pertain specifically to ones cultural practices. They are the aakhu that established the way you, your family, your extended family, etc. do the things that you do for so long and for so many generations. The cultural aakhu of many of African descendants in the Americas are honored as an old African man and woman called Papa Joe (Uncle or Uncle Joe) and Mother (Big Momma or Auntie). These cultural aakhu also called El Negro Jose and La Madama (or La Negra) in some of the Afro-Latin traditions and Mexican Spiritism. Other times they are called Francisco and Francisca in the Afro-Cuban practices or the Pretos Velhos in the Afro-Brazilian traditions, represent the first Africans brought from the Kongo-Angolan region, of one's lineage that were brought to the Americas. It is these Africans who were responsible for retaining and maintaining the African beliefs, practices and values, which continues to exist today and have a major influence on society.

- **Native American Aakhu,** are the spirits of Amerindians (Powatan, Cherokee, Seminole, Creek, Mohawk, Arawak, Taino Incas, Mayan, and many other Indian nations) who are the original caretakers of the Americas. Native American aakhu are honored for two reasons. The first is because it is a good practice to always honor and respect the ancestral spirits of the land you are upon. This is *maa* and the same is expected if you were to visit Hawaii or any other country. Just like you wouldn't go into another house and disrespect them. You do not go to another's country and disrespect the ancestral spirits there.

The second reason why Amerindian aakhu are honored is because even though Native American spirituality is different from African spirituality. There were more similarities that existed than differences, which resulted in a number of Native Americans assisting many African descendants during slavery by sheltering, hiding, intermarrying with them and even adopting runaways into their tribes throughout the Americas. As a result, Amerindian aakhu are honored because of their concern for the environment, defiant attitude and courageous free spirit, inspire self-defiance and justice. There are many Native American aakhu that exist, but the most popular Native American aakhu in North America are Black Hawk and Grey Hawk.

- **Mythical Aakhu,** are aakhu composed of prophets and biblical spirits such as Abraham, Queen Esther, King David and Solomon. The most popular mythical aakhu in many Afrospiritual traditions is Moses who inspired countless Abolitionists and Civil Rights leaders like Fredrick Douglas, Harriet Tubman and Dr. Martin L. King Jr.

- **Teaching Aakhu,** are educated or learned aakhu that gravitate towards us because of your chosen profession, interests in a particular vocation, etc. There are numerous teaching aakhu, as I mentioned before, when I discovered that Albert Einstein use to thank all of the deceased mathematicians that came before him. It became apparent to me he did this because they were the ones he believed helped him to make his discovery of relativity. It was through him that I got a better understanding of how aakhu function in our life and learned that one can have an aakhu from another cultures and ethnic group.

The Netcharu: The Guardian Spirits

If the living remembers the deceased as being an exceptionally benevolent individual in life and the deceased moves to the KAMTA. Then they choose to reincarnate to the land of the living and due to the lightness of their *ab* they are able to return to KAMTA again. And, they continue to repeat this same process numerous times. These spirits are said to have transcended beyond the birth-life-death-rebirth cycle, to the point that they have become totally resistant to the transformation

115

process. And have chosen to settle as forces of nature or angelic being called a netcharu.

The netcharu manifest themselves physically as large stones, roots, rivers and streams. The more remote the netcharu, the more immovable and permanent they are in nature. For instance, a fairly young netcharu might manifest itself as a smooth stone, whereas a great and very old netcharu may manifest itself as a boulder of some sort. Although some people may believe that these guardian spirits do not reveal themselves to us unless we are in danger, the truth is that any time we see something catch our eye. We just saw a glimpse of this spirit. They can be found everywhere and in every natural phenomenon that exists. Many are usually found wherever there is maa aankh (crossroad) that occurs because it is where two worlds meet.

The reason the netcharu resides in these places of nature is so that they can fulfill their role as a guardian and protectors over the natural resources of the planet. The netcharu therefore are the original masters of all skills and technologies (agriculture, architecture, hunting, medicine, etc.) and are the ones responsible for teaching the living how to live in harmony with the forces of nature in order to maintain the *maa* of the planet. This explains why Africa being the birthplace of humanity was the first continent to produce a civilization. It is because the people there developed a close relationship with the netcharu of the land. When people migrated out of Africa, many of them took the netcharu with them to these distant lands, which is why one can find a host of similarities between all cultures. This supports my belief that the netcharu are the original founders of the people, leaders of clans and rulers of kingdoms, which makes them the spiritual parents of us all whether we choose to believe in them or not.

Like parents they can strict, rough and demanding sometimes and other times be gentle and mild, because they can see our potential. Lacking a physical body they have the ability to put people in your path so that they can help you out of any jam as they had done with me regarding Ms. B, Papa and Iya. They will help you overcome any hardship because like any good parent they want us to grow, become wiser and live a righteous life.

116

Like Napoleon Hill's (Nine) Invisible Counselors, everyone has nine netcharu that walk with them and they are:

Osar

Osar was called upon whenever one wants justice, wisdom, assistance with fatherhood, peace, prosperity, a cool head or needs help in overcoming things that obscure one's clarity such as drugs, alcohol, etc. He is called upon by offering him anything white such as milk, rice, potatoes, boiled yucca, etc. but never any alcoholic beverage. It was understood that whenever one saw white animals (e.g. white doves, white dogs, etc.) or people in all white, that Osar was answering their petition. All days are sacred to Osar but he has an affinity for Sunday, which is his son's day. All the planets are sacred to Osar as well. Since, Osar is the foundation of everything, he lies underground. Avalanches, earthquakes, etc. are seen as attempts made by Set to usurp his throne. Praise Phrase: "Thank you Osar for peace, prosperity and wisdom."

Oset

Oset was petitioned whenever one needed assistance from strangers, had problems with the family, issues revolving around pregnancy, assistance with motherhood/nurturance, fertility issues, and patience. Her colors are blue and white or blue and silver. She loves melons, pineapples, seashells, fishing nets, fish, molasses, beer and rum. She is very fond of toy sailboats and model ships, which remind her of her voyage across the mystical waters of Nyun to find Osar and conceive a child. She speaks to us through seagulls, swallows, scorpions (according to one story she was protected by them), mature women (especially pregnant mothers) and children. Her celestial body is the moon (especially the waxing moon). Her sacred day is Monday (Moon-day). She is the patroness of women, mothers, single mothers and fisherman. Oset is the Mother of us All and the Queen of the Nation. Praise Phrase: "Thank you Oset for love, nurturance and protection."

Npu

Npu is called upon whenever one wants to find lost and hidden objects, find a way out no way and needs personal protection. The personal guardian of everyone is petitioned with rum, candy, cigar tobacco, toys, fruit and anything that is red, white and black. The Lord of the Roads and master of crossroads communicates to us mostly with dogs and canines. Npus prefer to sit next to doors with Hruaakhuti and Maat. When working with Npu, you must be specific and let him know what you want. If you leave it to his interpretation, you're most likely to have an adventure on your hands. Npu's sacred day is Wednesday and his celestial body is Mercury. Praise Phrase: "Guardian spirit of us all. Thank you for guiding me and Opening the Way."

Nebhet

Nebhet – the ex-wife of Set (believed to have married Hru after the Great War) is the guardian of love, happiness, sensuality and beauty. She is associated with Queen Esther and Mary Magdalene. Totem animal used to communicate messages with are usually cats, peacocks, and other graceful animals. Her colors are yellow and amber, as well as pink. She is fond of rum, champagne, beer, oranges, cantaloupes and honey. Nebhet's sacred day is Friday and celestial body is Venus. Praise Phrase: "Thank you Nebhet for love, success and happiness."

Hru

Hru – the true heir of Osar and son of Oset is the lord of thunder, the essence of maleness, who teaches self-control, courage and strategy. Hru's bravery, confidence, passion, strategic skills and success acquired through humility makes him associated with the biblical King David. Totem animal used to communicate messages with are hawks, rams and bulls. His colors are red and white or and sometimes the color brown. He is fond of rum, beer, and red wine and spicy foods. Hru is the patron of firemen, managers, supervisors, young men and all who need to be reminded to remember the consequences of their actions. Hru's sacred day is Sunday and his celestial body is the Sun. Praise Phrase: "Thank you for helping me to claim the victory over the enemy."

Djahuti

Djahuti – the vizier of Osar and the only one, who could see through Set's deception, is the guardian of wisdom and forms of divination including the sortilege system used in the Bible called *lots*. He is associated with King Solomon the wisest man of the Bible. Totem animal used to communicate messages with are storks, cranes and owls (indicating that if one does not change their life death is near). His colors are dark blue and white and he accepts the same gifts offered to Osar. Praise Phrase: "Thank you for repairing the Eye and helping me to See, Djahuti."

Hruaakhuti

Hruaakhuti the first to fight the energy but needed Hru's help to defeat the devil on battlefield is called upon for protection and the removal of obstructions created by Set. He is master of hard work and is offered for his assistance iron objects, which he is fond of, and anything that is blood red. He enjoys strong liquors including rum, gin, vodka and whiskey. He also is fond of strong cigars, roasted root vegetables, wild game and anything that outdoorsmen enjoy. Hruaakhuti's quick temperedness, hard work and fearless attitude is associated with the Apostle Peter. He is the patron of soldiers, guerilla fighters and warriors. Hruaakhuti is called upon anytime there is a battle, competition or struggle. He will fight endlessly, which is why he needs Hru to lend him a hand in order to defeat Set. Hruaakhuti's sacred day is Tuesday and his celestial body is Mars. Praise Phrase: "Thank you for protecting me from danger seen and unseen."

Maat

Maat is the personification of the maa, is responsible for helping us to establish balance, find peace and live a righteous life. She is the interpreter and protector of the law and guardian over nature. Maat is the patron of police and guards. Her colors are blue and yellow. She is fond of rum or water She is associated with John the Baptist. She is petitioned any time one needs help making sense of things or needs to find their bearings. Maat's sacred day is Thursday and her celestial body is Jupiter. Praise Phrase: "Thank you for bringing balance, order and justice into my life."

Sokar

Sokar is the guardian of the cemeteries, patron of the ill, wretched and the forgotten. Associated with Lazarus, Sokar takes the affliction, anguish, grief, misery, pain, suffering and all of the signs of decay and death (left at the gravesite/cemetery). Then he transforms them into our greatest strengths. Totem animal used to communicate messages with is an owl, vulture and sometimes, feral dogs. His colors are white, indigo, brown or purple. He is fond of rum, cigars, dry white wines, sesame seeds, dates and raisins. Sokar's sacred day is Saturday and celestial body is Saturn. Praise Phrase: "Thank you Sokar for health, strength and rebirth."

One thing that needs to be understood about the netcharu is that just like your aakhu. Your netcharu may be similar to the one's explained here but they are totally unique to you in their own special way. For instance, your Npu may prefer a pipe tobacco whereas another may prefer a strong cigar. Some of your netcharu may prefer for you to honor them in their Catholic guise to help nurture one's faith in order for them to get a better understanding of how KAMTA operates. Then some of your netcharu prefer for you not to honor them at all because they see your progress and feel that you are not ready yet. These ambiguities and differences exist because the netcharu that walks with us is actually a representative of an older essence. So, don't expect all of the spirits to be exactly the same.

How did these individuals became netcharu and Set became the ousted netchar is explained in the *Story of Osar.*

The Story of Osar
(Original rendering of a traditional legend)

The Age of Ra

It is said that in the beginning, Ra – *The Lord of Life and the Midday Sun* – was the first ruler of the two lands[15]. People honored their ruler Ra as he passed throughout the two lands, but monstrous and gigantic beasts often tried to usurp him. Several brave individuals rose in Ra's defense. One of the first was Nebhet known by her warrior name the lioness Sekmet, whose rage against the enemies of Ra was said to be so wild and uncontrollable. That she had to be tricked into drinking ale had to dyed red to resemble blood in her for her lull her back into senses.

Another great warrior that had risen to fight in Ra's honor was a warrior from Behutet known as Hru-Behutet (Hru of Behutet), Hruur (Hru the Elder) or simply Hruaakhuti (Hru of the Double Horizon), who was the first to create iron and later became the owner tools and weapons. But, in the end, Ra had tired of his subjects plotting for his demise so he ascended into the heavens. There he could still observe humankind and when the faithful needed him. They could go up high and call upon him, but in his absence he decided that Geb should rule the two lands.

The Age of Geb

Geb, the Lord of the Earth known today as Mother Nature – like Ra ruled the two lands with a firm arm. He was well received in the beginning because early human beings had learned how to make use of the natural resources available to them. Early human beings had gathered into groups and learned how to protect themselves from the beast of prey by creating crude weapons. With these weapons early

---

[15] Remember on the maa aankh, Ra corresponds to man and woman's paleo-mammalian brain, emotions, animal instincts, etc.

121

man learned eventually how to hunt as the women learned how to gathered foodstuff from the environment, but in a relatively short time. With limited natural resources available a war erupted amongst early human beings. Geb was often called upon to remedy the skirmishes that had erupted but was unable to do so. Having no other choice, Geb called a meeting amongst his children believed to be the tribal clan leaders of men, and he decided amongst Osar, Oset, Hru-ur, Nebhet and Set. That Set and his wife Nebhet the youngest of his children would rule the northern territory, while Osar and Oset the oldest of the children would govern the southern region. Hruur or Hruaakhuti was charged with maintaining the peace between the two.

The Age of Osar

When Osar became ruler of the southern land, (in some versions of the story) it is said Osar desiring to bring peace amongst the people went into the mountains to speak with Ra. Upon, his return he introduced a set of teachings to the people. Through these teaching a body of laws were created that the people used to self-govern themselves with. According to history and legend, the teachings were so influential and powerful that they spread like wildfire as Osar traveled the land teaching them. Shortly after, he learned from Oset how to cultivate plants and he began teaching his people agriculture.

Through agriculture, people began to trade as the teachings of Osar continued to spread throughout both lands. All loved Osar and cherished their beloved ruler because he brought peace and prosperity to all, and had succeeded in uniting the two lands. It was through his efforts he became ruler of both lands and the King of Kamit. Everyone loved Osar and honored him wherever he went but unknown to them all. Set had become very jealous of Osar's success and fame. So, when Osar decided to teach his teachings to others throughout the world and left with a company of dancers and entertainers on a world tour. In his fatherly absence, he decided to leave his faithful and loving wife Oset, the queen of the country in charge.

122

While Osar was away, Oset ruled the two lands perfectly but unknown to her or any of the followers of Osar. Set, was devising of a plan with several conspirators to murder Osar upon his return.

When Osar returned back from his tour. Set welcomed his unsuspecting brother and all the dignitaries of the kingdom with a great celebration in his honor. When all was full and merry with ale Set presented a beautifully decorated chest and promised to give it to whoever fit perfectly inside. No one had ever seen a chest like this so, one by one each of the guests tried to fit inside the chest but no one could. Set who knew all along that the chest would fit Osar coaxed Osar to lie down in the chest, which fit him perfectly. When Osar tried to regain his stance Set and his conspirators nailed the lid shut, and poured molten lead on the chest, thereby suffocating and killing Osar. Immediately afterwards, Set's conspirators threw the chest into the Nile. No one stood against Set as he usurped the throne. Not even the great Ra who wept of the news of Osar's death.

As expected, Set ruled the kingdom with an iron fist. He changed all of the laws that were erected and destroyed all memory of Osar's reign. He replaced "right" with "might" and made justice only beneficial to a few. Those who were loyal to Osar were inhumanely murdered, driven underground or out of the country. Hruaakhuti was the first to oppose Set, but Set was too powerful and eventually forced the old warrior to surrender under his sway, which is how Set became the Lord of War.

Set became an uncontrollable force that no one could stand against. No one opposed him, not even the first king Ra, because although he did not agree with Set. Ra – the Lord of Life and the Midday Sun, was also the governor of might and could find no wrong in what Set was doing. So since no one opposed him, he immediately he sent forth his agents to capture Oset.

But, when Oset heard the news of Osar's death, she immediately cut a lock of her hair. She then disguised herself by putting on mourning clothes and went in search for Osar's body to give him a proper burial. Secretly she searched high and low because she

123

was now a fugitive in her own land and abroad. Unable to find the chest, Ra - the Lord of Life and the Midday Sun – having pity upon her sent forth Npu to assist her.

Npu led Oset to come across a group of children who told her that they saw the chest floating out towards sea. So Oset took a small boat and set sail to Byblos. There she found a magnificent tree that had grown and had the chest containing the body of Osar inside. After pleading with the king of Byblos, who had cut down the tree and made the trunk into a pillar for his palace, for the chest. Oset took the chest and returned back to Kamit. Full of sorrow, Oset opened the chest and using magic she changed herself into a swallow. While hovering over the dead body, using her wings she caused his weary member to raise and impregnate her so that she could give birth to an heir. After receiving Osar's seed she transformed herself back into human form.

Secretly the pregnant Oset traveled back to her land to give birth to Osar's heir. Before doing so, she hid the chest containing the body of Osar in the marsh. While away in a nearby town preparing to give birth, Set during a hunting expedition found the chest and in a fit of rage. Hacked the body of Osar into 14 pieces and scattered it throughout the country. When Oset returned and found what Set had done, she once again guided by Npu and while carrying Hru, searched for the missing body parts of Osar, but this time. Apparently angered by Set's rage, Nebhet left Set and joined Oset in her quest.

Together they searched everywhere for the pieces of Osar's body and everywhere where they found a piece. They created a shrine informing people that here is where one of Osar's body parts was found. Thus advertising and reminding the people of Kamit how peaceful and prosperous the kingdom was when Osar was king. It wasn't long after, that all of the body parts of Osar were recovered except for his genitals, which were swallowed by a fish believed to be an agent of Set.

Now, Oset was still very saddened by the lost of her husband and she mourned heavily over Osar's lifeless body. Wishing that he returned she asked Djahuti if he could bring Osar back to life. Djahuti

124

knowing that Osar's spirit had departed from his body a long time ago knew that it would be difficult because Osar's spirit may not recognize the deformed body now. After searching for a way, Djahuti instructed that Osar's body be wrapped in linen and be given a proper burial ceremony, so that Osar could finally be allowed to rest in peace and exist forever as the first honorable ancestor.

The Rise of a Hero

There were many attempts made on the young Hru's life. Fortunately, none were successful, so when the young prince, son of Osar and Oset came of age. He was visited by Osar in a dream to avenge his father's wrongful death. As imagined, fueled by fury and vengeance, the impetuous youth boldly gathered a band of rebels and challenged his uncle for the throne. Set however, being older and more knowledgeable of war, for he was the author of war, engaged Hru and his band of rebels on the battlefield, but the battle between the two usually ended in a stalemate. We neither side able to clearly claim victory. Then in one major battle, Set had managed to get close enough to the young prince that he was able to gouge one of his eyes out, forcing Hru to retreat to his father's ex-vizier Djahuti.

Djahuti repaired magically Hru's eye, which gave the young warrior keen sight on how to defeat Set on the battlefield. With his eye repaired and new recruits, Hru met Set on the battlefield again, but this time he quickly and swiftly defeated his uncle by cutting Set at the seat of his pants, thus making him Set an eunuch. Hru then dragged Set, wounded and defeated to be judged by his mother Oset. But, Oset feeling pity for Set told Hru to free him and let him go. Angered by his mother's decision Hru cut off Oset's crown and stormed off in disgust.

Set, like most great enemies stated that Hru was not the true heir of Osar and proclaimed that he was a bastard. He then demanded that a tribunal be called so that he could be declared the true ruler of the kingdom. So, upon his request the two stood before a tribunal each pleading their case but when it came time for a judgment to be handed down. Some of the tribunal sided with Set and others decided with Hru, resulting in them not being able to reach a just decision and end the Great War.

The arguing and bickering between the tribunal members went on as long as the war had done. Until one day, Djahuti suggested to the tribunal that Osar as Tum speak from beyond the grave. When Osar (Tum) spoke he expressed his disappointment in the members for not being able to reach a fair decision. He reminded the tribunal that he was the one that taught and civilized the people of their wicked ways. That the barley that they grew and the cattle that they had, he taught them all how to become prosperous. In other words, Osar knew right from wrong, knew what worked and didn't work because he was right alongside them practicing what he preached. Osar didn't say one thing and do another because he was not a hypocrite. Everything that he said, he knew because he did it as well based upon his knowledge of the Spirit.

Osar gave thanks to God for establishing the Halls of Justice in the Underworld and that due to the maa being cast down by Set, thus making life unfair. Osar because of his ethical and moral accomplishments in the living world would reestablish the maa in the Underworld and become the first Lord of the Living and the Lord of the Dead. Osar then told the tribunal that as Lord of the Underworld, he had at his disposal the great devourer, which was part leopard (or lion), hippopotamus and crocodile called Aummit, whom at will. Osar would send to fetch the heart of anyone, so they better judge wisely or justly, because in the end. He would be their judge.

Based upon the words of Osar, the tribunal ruled in Hru's favor. Set was punished and forced to be a donkey that carries the very thing that could save him and bring him eternal life (the teachings of Osar), while Hru on the other hand was declared the victor because he was found to be *maakhru* "true of voice".

It was after experiencing grave misfortune, suffering the loss of his heritage, humiliation from his initial loss to Set and falling victim to Set's false accusations. That Hru was vindicated and awarded the white Hedjet crown, the Southern Crown of Kamit, signifying coolness, wisdom, purity, innocence, prosperity, perfect justice and all of the ideals of Osar. After unifying the two lands, Hru rebuilt all of his ancestors' temples that were destroyed by Set, and to commemorate his victory over evil, new temples were erected in his honor.

Why Is It Important to Honor the Netcharu?

Every time there is a peaceful event sponsored by Osar. Nebhet who is in charge of the festivities, invites everyone because she wants everyone to get along and enjoy themselves. But, whenever there is an accident, argument, fight, any type of chaos and confusion, disaster, storm, etc. It is because Set and the aapepu have crashed the event. It is usually Npu who is the first to see Set and the aapepu appear but the first netchar to respond to their calamity is usually Hruaakhuti, whether it is in a dance club or a natural disaster. When the skirmish between the two brothers cannot be quelled quietly and inconspicuously, Hru can usually be heard thundering across the sky or taking charge and demanding that Set retreats. Once Set has been forced to leave, Maat seeks to restore balance and order, while Sokar can be found trying to restore and reestablish a type of normalcy. As Oset tends to the wounded, Djahuti ponders on how to prevent such a situation from ever occurring again.

The reason it is important to honor the netcharu as you can see is because by doing so. You are able to identify with them and see how your netcharu manifest them selves in nature and within your being. By personifying your netcharu you build a rapport with them and that's when you begin to receive messages from God through them like warnings about danger. For example, one day my wife and I were meeting some people we knew in a nearby town. As we were driving I kept seeing hawks. The hawks were either perched up on the telephone post or flying alongside the car as we were driving. I knew that hawks were the totem animals of Hru but I didn't understand the message I was being given. I did however remain observant as I imagined Hru would have and I continued to follow the omens. When we finally arrived at the house of the people we were supposed to be meeting.

Something just seemed a little off. I couldn't put a finger on it but I felt a little funny.

Anyway, as the day progressed along, we ate some food and there was a conversation among a couple of people that had begun. My wife had left and was in a nearby room for a while so I went to go check on her to see if she was okay. The next thing I knew. The conversation between the two people had turned into a yelling match and finally into a full-fledge argument. I mean it happened so fast, that it was hard to believe. In five minutes, just about everyone that was there had left as if there was an evacuation. Thankfully, there were no serious altercations but clearly, Set was present. It wasn't until my wife and I after trying to tend to the host of the event, left to return home that it dawned on me. That Nebertcher sent Hru to tell me to be observant, watch my tongue, and keep a cool head.

As you can see, by developing a rapport with the netcharu you can learn how to recognize the signs and greatly improve your relationship with the Divine. The great thing about the relationship between you and the netcharu is that it allows you to distinguish between spiritual truths and superstitions. As well as prevents you from go down a destructive path inspired by self-deception and self-delusion.

Study Questions

1. What are angels?
   Angels are what most people from around the world call deities, gods, goddesses, daemons, to forms and archetypes. They are for the most part spiritual messengers.

2. Are angels higher and over man and woman?
   No. Man and woman were created in the image of God, which means angels are supposed to assist us in our life.

3. Even though a number of people believe in guardian angels, why don't most people know how to communicate with them?

Most people do not know how to communicate with their guardian angels because many have been discouraged from learning how to develop their *ab*, so that they can access their *ba*.

4. How do you access your *ba* so that you can communicate with your guardian angels?
   To communicate with your guardian angels you have to move your ab to the Amun Ra moment so that you can access your ba and enter KAMTA.

5. Are the guardian angels and other spirits a figment of our imagination?
   No. The various spirits exist on another plane. We are able to communicate with them with our imagination.

6. What does it mean if the ab of a spirit is very heavy and how does this spirit affect the living?
   If the ab of a spirit is very heavy it may mean that this spirit has a heavy heart and little to no conscience. Such a spirit is called an aapepu because these ghost like leech, suck the life out of the living by encourage us to follow in their unwise, destructive and negative footsteps.

7. Why are the aapepu considered to be dangerous?
   The aapepu are dangerous because in life they were confused, misguided and made horrible decisions. In death they have the ability to encourage the living (especially those who are ill, vulnerable, depressed and spiritually weak) to make the same type of choices, which leads to accidents, arguments, confusion, illness and even death.

8. What makes the aakhu uniquely different from aapepu?
   The aakhu are uniquely different from the aapepu because they have lived a courageous, self-disciplined and righteous life. They were selfless individuals in life that made sacrifices for the benefit of their family, community, people, etc. Whereas the aapepu through generally had no real concern for others, so

129

they preyed upon others (like beast do) for their own selfish benefit and gratification.

9. Who are the true followers of Set or devil worshippers?
   The true followers of Set are anyone that purposely uses their authority to abuse, exploit and profit from another's misery and suffering.

10. Why do people all over the world veneration their ancestors by commemorating them on special days, so widely practiced all over the world, even by people that through the building of monuments, memorials, masquerades, parades, etc.?
    Ancestor veneration is practiced worldwide because; God finds no fault with this practice that reminds the living that righteous living guarantees eternal life.

Exercise: How to Create Sacred Space

There has been a gross misunderstanding in how to improve one's life in recent years because. There has been a movement advocating that all one has to do is wish for the things they want, and it will magically appear before their eyes. It is suggested that all one has to do is to hold firmly in their mind's eye their objective and one's higher self, super conscious, higher intelligence, genii or god. Will cause whatever it is that the individual wants to physically manifest. While it is true that the use of the will is needed to bring spiritual energies into physical being, the process to do so is more involved and requires more than just concentration. Case in point, one can imagine to their heart's desire the conception of a baby, but unless a potent male and fertile female actually come together in unison, life will not be created.

In order for spiritual energies to manifest themselves physically, there has to be a bridge that unites both realms. This bridge only exists when we work with those on the other side. The way to unite both realms in order to work for a common goal one builds a spiritual altar.

The spiritual altar used in this practice draws its inspiration from the Afro-Cuban Espiritismo Cruzado practice for a number of reasons. The first reason is that it is a flexible altar used by many Bantu inspired traditions throughout the Americas as well as in Central and South African traditions. Second, this altar can easily be used by the solitary practitioner as well as within a group setting. Third, this spiritual altar can easily be adapted to one's beliefs, and finally. Forth, it is a remarkable multi-purpose altar that simply evolves through the use of your intuition or according to way things feel. If for instance, you feel that something doesn't seem right you simply remove it. If you choose to add something then you do so.

To construct this altar, make off your space with white seashells (or white rocks). Then place on the wall above where the altar will be built, a cross to symbolize the abstractness of Nebertcher as the Lord of Everything. Now, stand another cross in the center of the altar to represent the maa aankh and the resurrection of the aakhu and netcharu on the other side. Then take nine glasses of cool water and dedicate them to the nine netcharu. To honor the cultural aakhu that made it possible for African beliefs, practices and values to survive. Place an image to represent your Papa Joe on the left side and an image of Big Momma on the right. Then place photos of your masculine aakhu on the left and on the right side photos of your female aakhu. Decorate the altar to resemble a home for your aakhu because it is their spiritual home. And, since it is considered a spiritual home for your aakhu and netcharu, it is encouraged that all offerings be placed on the altar, unless your aakhu or netcharu reveals otherwise.

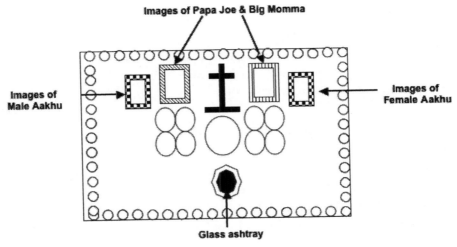

131

Why Dissimulate?

Now there are some that will ask why have I included the names other traditions in this practice. It is because, although we are in the 21st century and most of the oppressive laws forbidding us from practicing our culture has been abolished. When you move outside of the major cultural hubs in New York, California and Florida, and into the heart of the United States. You'll find that even though these laws have been destroyed, oppressive practices continue to exist. So what do you do when you live in the heart of the "Bible Belt?" You have to dissimulate your beliefs and fortunately for our sake, African thinking being circular (and not linear) has survived thus far by simply adapting, bending, borrowing and disguising itself amongst other artifacts in order to protect itself from prying eyes.

Now, I must admit that at first I didn't agree with this practice. In fact, I use to think that by camouflaging our Africanness one was "selling out." Until, I learned that the figurines simply symbolize the universal spiritual energy and are used to help one understand the dynamics of the spiritual realm. El Niño de Atocha for instance, is Npu in the Catholic tradition and Joseph (Yosef) the Dreamer in the Hebrew tradition, but it is the same netchar Npu just expressed in different ways.

By representing the netcharu using various icons is not selling out at all. It simply reflects the maturity of your faith, because through this array of icons others are able to get a better understanding of the netcharu as well. So by representing Npu as El Niño de Atocha, one is able to see the optimistic nature of Npu and call upon Npu to open the way when situations seem impossible.

Two Story Spiritual House

If you choose to honor the netcharu think of their space as being like a spiritual home as well. If using a shelf, which is optimal and preferred. Most of the netcharu (except for Npu, Maat and Hruaakhuti which I will explain later) can share the second shelf and use it like the second floor of a home. The analogy is simple. Occupying the first floor, are our aakhu but on the second floor is where the guest or the netcharu reside. The icons of the netcharu should always be kept in a clay pot to provide the netcharu with its own separate space. These clay pots are like the rooms of the netcharu and should be decorated according to the nethar's specifications. For example, if you are inspired to make a guest room (clay pot) for Oset. Possible items she may want to remind you that she is the netcharu that searched for Osar, is associated with pregnancy and the ocean are: a sailboat (used to travel to Syria to retrieve Osar's body), seashells, fishing nets, a miniature skull honoring those that jumped into the ocean during slavery, etc. For designs, ask your aakhu for guidance and follow your intuition.

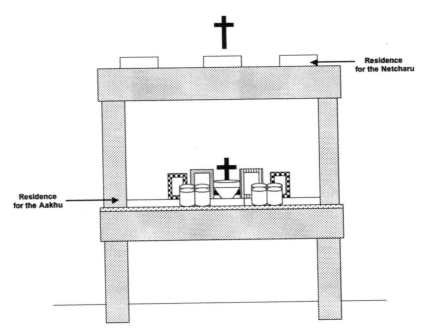

The spiritual pots for Npu, Maat and Hruaakhuti should be kept near the front door of your home (if possible) or near an entrance and always near the floor, because they are warriors and warriors like to sit near the ground. If desired Hruaakhuti will usually request an iron pot instead of a clay pot.

Because the aakhu and netcharu are spiritual forces they do not need to consume food and drink in order to maintain their body. They do however need energy and they are able to absorb the energy of physical things that are offered to them. Some of the most common offerings that are given are:

- Candles – all colors and types. White candles are usually offered for devotional purposes and general offerings.
- Incense – the smoke of incense transports petitions to the spiritual realm. The most commonly used incense is frankincense to attract high spirits and sandalwood that attracts all spirits.
- Colognes – spirits are also fond of colognes and perfumes, especially Bay Rum and Florida Water.
- Fresh Flowers – remind the spirits of the beauty and love experienced in life. Trust your intuition as to which flowers to offer.
- Black coffee – is usually offered to the aakhu and never with sugar to make them more alert. I find it beneficial to offer them coffee in the evening my time, which is the morning their time.
- Alcoholic beverages – beer, liquor (whiskey, rum, etc.) and wine, are favorite offerings of the aakhu and netcharu, but only give them enough to quench their thirst and not enough to get them drunk. And, never ever ever, give Osar any alcoholic beverage.
- Tobacco – cigar smoke is a spiritual fuel for the aakhu and netcharu. Every spiritual altar that I have seen such as those in the Afrospiritual tradition to the Chinese and Vietnamese home altars, they all have spirits that like tobacco smoke. To offer cigar smoke takes practice because it involves you putting the lit end in your mouth and blowing the smoke out of the opening, so that the spirits puff the smoke. Be careful not to burn yourself. If you do not wish to smell the smoke of the cigar. You can simply tell your spirits and just offer them an unlit cigar.
- Money – sometimes spirits will accept money. To offer money simply put the money in a special dish and leave it for them as

payment. When you offer the spirits money do not take it back and use it for something else. This is disrespectful and not maa.

- Fruit and Sweets – fruit reminds spirits of the bountiful life and sweets like cookies, cakes and candies remind spirits of the sweetness of life. Aakhu are fond of peppermint candies, while most Npus enjoy candies that children are fond of.
- Cooked Food – such as food that the aakhu enjoyed while alive can be offered, but it must be cooked with no salt. Spirits have an adverse reaction to salt, which repels them wherever there is salt. Whenever cook food is offered it must be removed shortly after so that it does not spoil. It can be consumed as is done in some cultures, placed in a garbage disposal, compost heap or thrown away. Simply follow your intuition and by all means use commonsense.

Knocking on the Ancestors' Door

To open communication with my aakhu and netcharu, sometimes I begin by reciting the *Lord's Prayer*, which is an excellent general, yet powerful prayer that puts me in the mindset that I am preparing to talk to God, my spiritual community leaders, spiritual clan heads and other spiritual dignitaries that have taken an interest in my life. Once my *ab* is at the Amun Ra moment (the right frame of mind/the magical and spiritual mindset), while looking at the crucifix above I express my gratitude to Nebertcher and thank the Lord of Everything for all my blessings by saying, "Thank Nebertcher for the aakhu and netcharu. I asked that you continue to bless them with power, strength and wisdom so that they can share it with me."

Since it is my aakhu that are closest to me and the ones who introduced me to the netcharu, I respectfully place on the altar a white candle and other offerings (such as black coffee, shot glass of rum and a cigar, etc.). I light the white candle and say, "Thank you aakhu, for your power, strength and wisdom. I ask that you continue to share your power, strength and wisdom with your child, so that I can continue improve my life." After greeting the aakhu, I follow the same procedure for those netcharu that have manifested, themselves to me. For instance, since Npu, Hruaakhuti and Maat are three netcharu that work closely together in our everyday life. After placing offerings that these particular netchar have asked for in front of their respective clay pots, I begin by offering Npu light, some candies and a shot of rum first because he has a tendency to wander off (like a curious child) if not taken care of. I then tell Npu, "Thank you Npu for opening the Way and guiding me safely to my destination." Next, I express my gratitude to Hruaakhuti by telling him, "Thank you Hruaakhuti for protecting me from danger seen and unseen," and finally Maat, "Thank you Maat for bringing balance and order into my life."

Then express your gratitude to your aakhu and ask that they share their knowledge and wisdom with you to improve the quality of your life. Tell them that you offer them light and water for their assistance. Next wait a few minutes for the aakhu to absorb the energy that has been offered. When you sense that they are ready. You can ask your question or tell them what is troubling you. Speak to them as if they were physically right in front of you in common day language. Then move your *ab* to the Amun Ra moment and wait for them to communicate to your *ba*.

Be aware of how the messages are revealed to you because this is usually how your spirits will communicate to you. A lot of times the aakhu will speak to you through your dreams and the netcharu will converse with you through some other medium like an animal that crosses your path or through a complete stranger.

Once you have received your answer tell them thank you. If you have not received your answer yet, tell them thank you still because they are working on your petition or request.

Close the door to your spirits' house by telling them thank you and extinguishing the candle that was lit for them.

There are only three hard rules that must be honored when working with this type of altar and they are:

1. Once you put the glasses on the altar you need to attend to it faithfully by never allowing it to decay. This means changing

the water at least once a week and if you put flowers on the altar. You need to replace them before they decay. If you cannot replace the flowers, it is better to not have flowers at all then to have dropping flowers all over the altar. The same applies for cook foods and alcoholic beverages that ripen because of the yeast in them.

2. Always offer your aakhu and netcharu light and cool water at least once a week. If you cannot offer them light then offer them an incense or tobacco smoke. And of course, **never leave the candles unattended** and near flammable surfaces.

3. Never put a photo of a living person on the spirits' altar. Remember, this is your spirits' home, which means that everyone in the house exists on the other side. If you wish that the aakhu and netcharu bless someone. Issue your request and offer them a candle for their assistance.

Protecting Your Dwelling From Aapepu

Occasionally, you will come in contact with some aapepu because as you develop and strengthen your *ab*. You will appear as a beacon of light to these negative spirits on the other side, like moths are to flame. As a result, they will be attracted to your spiritual altar. Other times, aapepu might attach themselves to you when you pass by places where their influence is strong like, haunted houses, alleyways, hospitals, cemeteries and other places where unfortunate circumstances have occurred. You will know when you have come in contact with them if they happen to catch your eye instantly and you begin to have negative thoughts or reaction for no apparent reason. Whatever the case, there is no need to be alarm because this is natural and most can be chased away. If you "knock" on the door of your aakhu and netcharu, it will overtime create a religious thoughtform that will discourage most aapepu. Some other ways will be discussed shortly.

Before explaining these different ways of protecting your space, it cannot be overstated the importance of maintaining your *ab*. The easiest way to prevent aapepu from entering your dwelling is by first and foremost observing your thoughts and protecting your *ab*. If you don't have control of your *ab* and you are not trying to strengthen it. No amount of physical protection is going to help you. Your best protection against the aapepu is to develop *self-control* and **self-discipline**. When you do it will be very difficult for any negative influence to move you because no one can make you do something that wasn't first in your heart.

Spirituality you must remember has nothing to do with practices and rites. Some of the most religious people in the world pray, chant and sing praises to God. Then as soon as church lets out or they leave the temple they return back to their hellish ways, because they believe in God but they don't know God. As stated in the beginning, believing in God means believing that God is outside of your being and distant from the whole of creation. When you know God, you know that God knows everything because God is within you. God simply gives you a choice to grow and become a god or goddess, or stay as a child. Those that choose to manifest miracles in their life, choose to become a more spiritual individual so that they can help others escape the suffering that they are in as well. When you have this strong conviction on your *ab*, aapepu won't even bother messing with you because the vibe you give off is that you are serious about your growth. This means that if an aapepu chooses to engage you, they will have a serious fight on their hand and would probably lose the little amount of energy (light) that they have. This is why aapepu leech upon those whom they see as being vulnerable.

So, the various protection remedies for your dwelling are for those who are serious about righteous living. Anyone can benefit from them, but if you are not serious about living righteously. It is like putting on makeup to cover an offensive odor (smile)... These physical protection remedies are simply an expression of your spiritual dedication. They are the outward appearance for your inner power and strength or a sign of intimidation. That informs all spirits that they if they are allies they are welcomed but if they enemies they better stay out until they are ready to evolve.

So the first protection remedy to guard against the aapepu is to place objects that encourage life and discourage negative influences. Pineapple plants, cactuses, pinecones, fresh pine needles and other plants with sharp and protruding edges facing outward are all very good protecting agents. Some plants like basil, spearmint and even some pepper plants, which are all common plants my wife's grandmother who was a *curandera* (Hispanic folk healer), kept are also good protective agents because of their scents.

All that is required is that you ask the plant to assist in protecting you and your dwelling. Offer the plant some water and follow your intuition. Remember to treat the plant with respect and in order to receive its assistance. If you take from a plant such as pinecone or pine needles be sure to offer something in return because it is the *maa* thing to do.

Some other ways to protect against aapepu is by placing miniature weapons or carefully arranging sharp objects like broken glass, nails, knives, needles, etc. and placing them near entrances. These can be put inside vases and put outside the front door. Animal parts like alligator heads, rattlesnake rattles, rattlesnake fangs, raccoon claws, bear claws, turtle shell, rooster nails, etc., which are all common items in Afro-Diaspora traditions, can also be used but these items had to be acquired in a correct manner.

If parts of these animals were acquired in a negative way, the part will be useful because the spirit of the animal was disrespected and improperly taken. This is not maa, nor is poaching and hunting just for sport. Our ancestors were agrarians. They farmed, fished and hunted for food, and thanked the Spirit for providing for them. They knew about the potency of certain animal parts like the roe of fish and the penis of a turtle because this what they hunted to live. They didn't just kill an animal just to get its bone or tusk, as is the case nowadays. They dependent upon the land and the land depended upon them. They did not encourage the abuse and misuse of natural resources. And, they certainly do not condone it. So, if you want a part of an animal, simply trust your intuition and allow the spirit of the animal to deliver it to you. When I did this, I obtained an alligator head, antlers and other animal parts from people that felt the need to give these objects to me.

A more clever and aesthetic method of protection is to purchase an image of an animal (or create your own) in an aggressive stance. Animals like roosters, cats, elephants, etc. can also be imbued with power to protect one's dwelling.

Conclusion

You have all been called but understand that accepting this calling doesn't mean that you will not be humiliated, excused from pain and will have no more suffering. It doesn't mean that just because you established a relationship with God through your aakhu and netcharu that all tat is wrong in your is going to miraculously and suddenly go away. No, but what it does mean, is that you're not alone and that your aakhu and netcharu will help you to overcome every difficulty that is in your path. Therefore, you don't need to worry. That's when this scripture popped into my mind, but was changed into a poem to reflect my new spiritual belief, which I am using here to conclude this book for those of called to follow this path.

And now
That you belong to Hru,
You are the true child of Osar
You are his heir,
And Now
All the promises that God promised him
Because of his righteous living
Belongs to you.
Amen.

INDEX

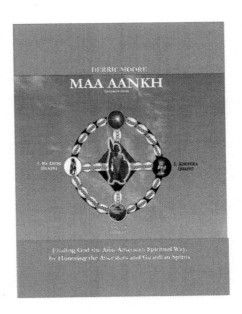

Maa Aankh Vol. I (2nd Edition): Finding God the Afro-American Spiritual Way, by Honoring the Ancestors and Guardian Spirits

Paperback: 358 pages   ISBN-13: 978-0985506728

He was pruned to be a preacher like his father, but when the Holy Ghost failed to save him from the drug related violence of the 1980s. He sought an alternative route and found the MAA AANKH, an Afro-American cosmology based upon Ancient Egyptian and Bantu-Kongo philosophy. In this unforgettable spiritual memoir, Moore reveals the roots of a spiritual tradition practiced in Central Africa, which originated in Ancient Egypt, as he fights his ignorance and skepticism of African spirituality, in order to overcome a generational curse, financial woes and the debilitating illness lupus.

Maa:
A Guide to the Kamitic Way for Personal Transformation

Paperback: 204 pages   **ISBN-13:** 978-0985506704

Before the 42 Laws of Maat and the 10 Maat Virtues, the ancient philosophers of Kamit (Egypt) relied upon a set of shamanic principles that taught how to work the Ra (the Spirit of God), called the Seven Codes of Maa. Like most shamanic principles the 7 Codes allowed the Kamitic people to see science and magic as the same thing, and work them both. In this book you will learn how to discover your purpose in life, reconnect to your ancestral past, create sacred spaces, and foretell the future using ordinary objects found in nature in order to change your dreams into a reality.

Maa Aankh Vol. II:
Discovering the Power of I AM
Using the Shamanic Principles of
Ancient Egypt for Self-Empowerment and
Personal Development

Paperback: 226 pages   **ISBN-13:** 978-0985506711

After learning that early African Americans in the Antebellum South followed the Kongo Cross, which the author used to discover the Maa Aankh, an Egyptian-style medicine wheel. Using this diagram as a guide revealed that the familiar physical reality we live in is limited, but beyond our five physical senses is a rich and unlimited spiritual dimension. Everything we desire – peace, prosperity, success, love, joy – can be found in this spiritual realm, because they are ethereal in nature. Most people have a problem obtaining these goals because they allow themselves to become disconnected from their Source. But, by learning how to stay connected to this invisible reality, you can overcome the physical problems you face. Included are practical exercises based upon shamanic traditions that will help you break away from the destructive beliefs and habits that disconnect you from the Source. As well as spiritual practices and rites that will help you maintain the connection to create the life that you want and deserve

Maa Aankh Vol. III:
The Kamitic Shaman Way of Working the Superconscious Mind to Improve Memory, Solve Problems Intuitively and Spiritually Grow Through the Power of the Spirits

Paperback: 236 pages   **ISBN-13:** 978-0985506742

Our current state of affairs is proof that if you want change, it is not enough to say you believe in God. In order to create change and make miracles occur in your life. You have to "know" you are made in the image of God and act on it! Once again, refusing to conform to any academic, religious or philosophical doctrine because it constitutes blind obedience. By using the Seven Codes of Maa (the core concepts and principles of ancient Egyptian spirituality), Moore has once again eloquently laid out a practical and scientific approach to Kamitic spirituality that any novice or adept would appreciate but, this time. He has gone a step further by showing how to implement the concepts and principles as an Afro-American healing art. In this informative and illustrated book, you will learn: * How to use the Superconscious mind to improve your memory and create miracles. * How to use the Superconscious mind to foresee the future using simple divination techniques. * How to establish a connection between your superconscious mind and the spiritual realm. * How to build altars, spirit pots and alternative altars (for those limited by time, space, unforeseen circumstances, etc.). * And, much, much more. Discover how to wake up the Divine within you and improve your life today!

Visit us at:
1SoLAlliance.com

For Maa Aankh cosmograms
and additional learning tools.

Help Get the Word Out!

I would like to personally thank you for purchasing the *Kamta: A Practical Kamitic Path for Obtaining Power* and reading it in its entirety. I hope that you enjoyed reading the strategies and techniques that I have shared with you in this book.

It would be immensely helpful to me if you could write a review for this book and publish it on Amazon.com.

To write a review:
1. Simply type in Amazon's search engine **Kamta**.
2. Scroll down to the reviews section.
3. And just write an honest review (good or bad) and give the book as many stars as you think it deserves.

Thank you in advance,

Derric "Rau Khu" Moore